Motivating the Millennial Knowledge Worker

Help today's workforce succeed in today's economy

Donald Shandler, Ph.D.

Contributing Experts

Rick Humphress
Oracle Corporation

Sue McLeod
Hay Group®

Shaara Roman
CGI Federal

Hector Velez
HireStrategy

Viva Books
New Delhi | Mumbai | Chennai | Kolkata
Bengaluru | Hyderabad | Kochi | Guwahati

First Indian Edition 2011

VIVA BOOKS PRIVATE LIMITED

- 4737/23 Ansari Road, Daryaganj, New Delhi 110 002
  E-mail: vivadelhi@vivagroupindia.net, Tel. 42242200
- 76, Service Industries, Shirvane, Sector 1, Nerul, Navi Mumbai 400 706
  E-mail: vivamumbai@vivagroupindia.net, Tel. 27721273, 27721274
- Jamals Fazal Chambers, 26 Greams Road, Chennai 600 006
  E-mail: vivachennai@vivagroupindia.net, Tel. 28290304, 28294241
- B-103, Jindal Towers, 21/1A/3 Darga Road, Kolkata 700 017
  E-mail: vivakolkata@vivagroupindia.net, Tel. 22836381, 22816713
- 7, Sovereign Park Apartments, 56-58, K. R. Road, Basavanagudi, Bengaluru 560 004
  E-mail: vivabangalore@vivagroupindia.net, Tel. 26607409, 26607410
- 101-102 Mughal Marc Aptt., 3-4-637 to 641, Narayanguda, Hyderabad 500 029
  E-mail: vivahyderabad@vivagroupindia.net, Tel. 27564481, 27564482
- First Floor, Beevi Towers, SRM Road, Kaloor, Kochi 682 018, Kerala
  E-mail: vivakochi@vivagroupindia.net, Tel: 0484-2403055, 2403056
- 232, GNB Road, Beside UCO Bank, Silpukhuri, Guwahati 781 003
  E-mail: vivaguwahati@vivagroupindia.net, Tel: 0361-2666386

www.vivagroupindia.com

Published by arrangement with

Axzo Press, LLC
562, Willow Brook Office Park
Fairport, New York 14450

ISBN : 978-81-309-1852-5

Published by Vinod Vasishtha for Viva Books Private Limited, 4737/23, Ansari Road, Daryaganj, New Delhi - 110 002. Printed and bound by Raj Press, R-3, Inderpuri, New Delhi - 110 012.

Table of Contents

About the Author

Dr. Shandler is president of Shandler Associates, a consulting firm that focuses on managing and motivating Millennials and assisting technical experts in transitioning into management and leadership roles. He has extensive experience working with multigenerational learners and knowledge workers in corporate, government, university, and association settings.

Holding a Ph.D. from Ohio State University, Shandler serves on the Board of Directors for the Northern Virginia Workforce Investment Board, the Greater Reston Chamber of Commerce, and the University of Maryland, Baltimore County, Instructional Systems Design Graduate Program. He is an alumnus of Leadership Fairfax and a recipient of the 2009 Outstanding Committee Chairperson Award from the Greater Reston Chamber of Commerce.

Previous books include *From Technical Specialist to Supervisor*, *Reengineering the Training Function: How to Align Training with the New Corporate Agenda,* and *Competency and the Learning Organization.* Further, he has presented seminars and speeches on these and other relevant topics nationwide.

Dr. Shandler encourages readers to share their organizations' challenges and solutions in motivating Millennials through his blog posted on www.motivatingmillennials.com. He is available for keynote speeches, executive briefings, and workshop presentations. He can be reached by e-mail at don@shandlerassociates.com or donaldshandler@comcast.net or by phone at 703.674.6800.

Acknowledgements

Special appreciation is extended to the Contributing Experts and their respective organizations for their efforts in helping me identify the key Millennial motivational factors that drove the contents of this book. Their willingness to share relevant practices and strategies enriched each chapter. In addition, I would like to thank Hector Velez for introducing me to many of the Contributing Experts, Shira Harrington for reviewing and commenting on each chapter, and finally, Monica Montoya for creating the Motivational Factors Survey Analysis, which harnessed data that influenced the structure of the book.

Further, I must acknowledge the outstanding research and publication efforts of the authors quoted in this book and whose names appear in the bibliography. They have created a significant and growing body of generational literature.

Last, I extend my sincerest appreciation to Axzo Press. Their editors and team of marketing and production professionals have helped bring this project from concept to print.

Contributing Experts

Lesley N. Channell
Assistant Vice President, Human Resources
HCA Northern Virginia Market
Dominion Hospital & Center

Lesley Channell is the assistant vice president of Human Resources at Reston Hospital Center and provides support for HCA's Northern Virginia market. Lesley has worked in healthcare for the last 16 years, with 13 years' experience in human resources. Lesley received her bachelor's degree from Ithaca College in Ithaca, New York, and earned her master's degree in business administration/human resources management from Iona College in New Rochelle, New York. She has been certified as a professional in human resources by the Society for Human Resource Management.

Jennell Evans
President and CEO
Strategic Interactions, Inc.

Jennell Evans is co-founder, President, and CEO of Strategic Interactions, Inc., an award-winning performance improvement firm in Vienna, Virginia. Jennell specializes in innovative corporate initiatives involving change communications, leadership development, and creative strategic planning.

She holds a BFA from Virginia Commonwealth University, a Certificate of Instructional Design, and a Masters of Organizational Development from Marymount University. Jennell is also certified to administer the Emotional Competency Inventory (ECI) and the Myers-Briggs Type Inventory (MBTI).

In addition to her work with clients, Jennell is actively engaged in community leadership programs and is Vice Chair of Leadership Fairfax, Inc.

Erin Nicole Gordon
Systems Integration
Accenture

Erin Nicole Gordon is a business analyst with the Reston, VA, office of Accenture. Involved in systems and integration technology consulting, Erin focuses on program management, proposal development, and SAP application solutions. She has muralled professionally and leads nonprofit efforts for numerous organizations, leading a missions teams internationally in 2009.

Her educational accomplishments include earning a B.S. in Commerce (International Business and Marketing concentrations) from the University of Virginia McIntire School of Commerce, and degrees in Spanish and Studio Art from the University of Virginia. Erin is a member of the National Scholars Honor Society.

Nicole Hardin
Managing Director
HireStrategy

Nicole Hardin is currently the Managing Director for HireStrategy. HireStrategy provides human capital solutions. HireStrategy, an *Inc*. 500 company, is ranked by *The Washington Business Journal* as the #1 regional staffing firm in the Greater Washington area.

Nicole has nine years' experience in assisting emerging-growth, mid-market, and *Fortune* 500 organizations build their human capital infrastructure and in managing the technology practice. For the past six years, she has assisted leading technology organizations in the D.C. community and been ranked in the top two technology recruiters from 2003 through 2005. Before working for HireStrategy, Nicole was the leading recruiter for NRI Staffing and Glotel, an international staffing firm.

Shira Harrington
Director, Professional Search
Positions Inc.

Shira Harrington, Director, Professional Search, at Positions Inc., is a frequent keynote speaker on managing the multigenerational workforce. As an outgrowth of her successful recruiting career, she brings her real-world perspective to help executives maximize the competencies of all four generations in order to create harmonious and robust workplaces. Shira's work has been published in monthly association magazines, and she has been profiled in the *Washington Business Journal*. An avid volunteer in the local HR community, she has served as VP of Programs for DC SHRM, is Programs Chair for the HR Leadership Forum, facilitates a monthly brown-bag meeting for Washington, D.C.–area HR professionals, and leads an executive peer roundtable for small-staff association executives. She earned her Masters in Public Relations from the University of Maryland at College Park.

Deborah K. Hoover
Director, Human Resources
The Urban Institute

Deborah K. Hoover, SPHR, is currently the Director of Human Resources for The Urban Institute, a Washington D.C. policy research institution. Ms. Hoover has worked within the nonprofit, academic, and research sectors for many years and is an active member of the HR professional community. She has served on the boards of the Human Resources Leadership Forum and the Washington Area Compensation and Benefits Association, and she participates in several HR-related work groups in the D.C. metro area.

Rick Humphress
Public Sector, Human Capital Management
Oracle Corporation

Rick Humphress has nearly 25 years' experience serving in a variety of individual contributor roles at such companies as Xerox, Motorola, INTERSOLV, and Oracle. He currently serves as an Oracle Human Capital Management specialist, advising international, federal, state, and local public-sector organizations on talent management issues. Rick has published articles on human performance improvement and competency modeling. He received a BA from Stanford and an MBA from Portland State, and he is working on a PhD from Walden University in Public Policy and Administration.

Kris T. Jensen
Vice President, Corporate Services
Wisdom Worker Solutions

Kris Jensen is the Vice President of Corporate Services for Wisdom Worker Solutions. She joined this startup in 2007 after eight years as the Senior Vice President of Human Resources for The Weitz Company, a $1.5 billion national commercial contractor. Before that, Kris spent 18 years with The Principal Financial Group, an international $45 billion financial services firm. She began her career there as a Life and Health Underwriter, but honed her craft as a human resources professional by assuming the leadership of Principal's employment, administrative, succession planning, training and development, Affirmative Action, and diversity functions.

Kris holds a Bachelors degree in Industrial Administration, Behavioral Management, from Iowa State University.

Peter W. Kennedy
Principal
The PRM Consulting Group

Peter Kennedy has had over 25 years of experience in conducting and managing compensation consulting projects for a variety of employers in the private, nonprofit, and public sectors. Peter has been a frequent speaker and panelist and has published numerous articles on the subject of compensation. He is the outgoing President of the Capital Area Chapter of the National Association of Corporate Directors.

Peter is a graduate of Oberlin College (BA in Government, 1975, with Honors) and the Sloan School of Management, M.I.T. (M.S.M. degree in economics and industrial relations, 1980).

Stacey Kessel
Senior Career Planning Manager
Booz Allen Hamilton

As the Senior Career Planning Manager at Booz Allen Hamilton, Stacey Kessel is responsible for delivering career planning resources and tools to employees and managers. Before joining Booz Allen, Stacey was the Associate Director of Career Services at Harvard Business School, where she counseled MBA students on their career searches. Stacey graduated from Colby College and has an MBA from the Kellogg Graduate School of Management at Northwestern University. Stacey has been interviewed by CNN, *Forbes*, and National Public Radio regarding the job search process.

Robert McGovern
CEO and Founder
Jobfox

Rob McGovern is a 20-year technology and media-industry veteran with a passion for helping people find careers they love. Before founding Jobfox, McGovern was the founder and former CEO of CareerBuilder. He grew CareerBuilder into a profitable $150 million company with more than 400 employees. His new venture, Jobfox, is already the fastest growing career site on the Web with precision matching and new Jobfox Intros™ services—the first online networking tools that make personal introductions between top-rated candidates and corporate recruiters.

McGovern is the author of a best-selling career advice book: *Bring Your "A" Game: The 10 Career Secrets of the High Achiever*. His expert career advice has been featured on numerous television and radio programs and in print and online publications throughout the world.

Before founding CareerBuilder, McGovern was vice president and general manager at Legent Corporation, the world's seventh-largest software company. He began his professional career at Hewlett Packard, where he rose through the sales and marketing ranks in both the United States and Europe.

Sue McLeod
Senior Consultant
Hay Group, Inc.

Sue McLeod started with a math degree and a job programming computers. In 22 years of working in technology consulting, she held various positions ranging from individual contributor to senior leader. Along the way, her interest in technology was eclipsed by a passion for helping people be more effective in organizations. Her second career in leadership development, assessment, and coaching allows her to fulfill those passions.

Sue works for Hay Group, Inc., in Arlington, Virginia. She lives with her partner, Ed, and her two Millennial-generation daughters. She knits compulsively in her spare time and dreams of ocean kayaking.

Kitty Nix
Director, Strategic Development
Helios HR

Kitty Nix's consulting and human resources experience spans 13 years, including leadership and management positions in two consulting firms. She is responsible for human resources and strategic development and was actively involved in business development, marketing, and daily operations for the consulting business. Kitty's technical HR expertise includes strategic planning for HR and organizational development. She holds an M.S. in Organizational Development from George Mason University and a B.S. in Computer Information Systems from James Madison University. She is certified as a Senior Professional of Human Resources (SPHR), received her Executive Leadership Coaching certificate from Georgetown, and was awarded one of the six 2007 HR Leadership Awards of Greater Washington.

Marcia Riley
Vice President, Talent Management and Human Resources
ESI International

In January 2008, Marcia B. Riley accepted the position of Vice President, Talent Management and Human Resources, at ESI International in Arlington, Virginia. Before joining ESI International, Marcia served as Assistant Vice President, Talent Management, and Chief Learning Officer for Inova Health System in Northern Virginia. Before that, she served as Senior Training and Development Executive for Sallie Mae.

Marcia's more than two decades of talent management experience also include leading her own consulting practice, which served a range of industries and organizations, including the U.S. Senate Office of Education and Training, The Nature Conservancy, Noblis, the Society of periOperative Registered Nurses, VeriSign, The American Press Institute, and The American Society of Training and Development. Marcia lives in Silver Spring, Maryland.

Shaara Roman
Director, Human Resources
CGI Federal

Shaara Roman is the Director of Human Resources for CGI Federal, a leading IT systems-integration and managed-services provider to the federal government and a wholly owned U.S. operating subsidiary of CGI Group, Inc. Ms. Roman is responsible for providing strategic HR direction and ownership of all HR functions for the 1700-member organization.

Ms. Roman honed her HR expertise over the past 15 years in varied corporate leadership roles in public and private organizations within the financial services and IT industries. Ms. Roman received her MBA in International Business from Georgetown University in Washington, D.C.

Christopher R. Ryan
Deputy General Counsel
K12 Inc.

Christopher R. Ryan currently serves as Vice President and Deputy General Counsel of K12 Inc., a leading provider of virtual education products and services. Prior to K12, Mr. Ryan served as General Counsel and Vice President of Human Resources at Everest Software, as Deputy General Counsel at CareerBuilder, and as Branch Chief at the SEC. Mr. Ryan earned a JD from American University, an MBA from the Smith School of Business at the University of Maryland, College Park, and a BA from Wake Forest University. Mr. Ryan is also a contributor to the book *The Worst-Case Scenario Survival Handbook: Work* by Joshua Piven.

Neil Sawyer
Senior Director of Human Resources
The Campagna Center

Neil Sawyer serves as Senior Director of Human Resources for The Campagna Center, a nonprofit organization serving the families and community of Alexandria, Virginia. He received his Masters in Human Resources Management from Marymount University. Neil has over 16 years of HR expertise in a wide variety of industries, including technology, construction, manufacturing, nonprofits and associations, and publishing. He is former President of the Washington, D.C., chapter of SHRM, and he remains active in HR lobbying and in mentoring new arrivals to the profession of human resources.

Kurt Schlimme
Project Management Office Director
The College Board

Kurt Schlimme is a business and technology executive with 15 years of managerial experience. Currently, Kurt is the Project Management Office Director at The College Board, overseeing the development of processes, practices, standards, and tools related to the execution of project-based work in IT. Before coming to The College Board, Kurt held the position of Vice President of Professional Services for iBasis Speech Solutions. Kurt was also a co-founder and Vice President of Strategic Solutions for the NDC Group, a management consulting firm that was purchased by PSInet in 2000, after growing from 10 to 350 employees.

Mark Steffanina
Director, Organizational Effectiveness
Holy Cross Hospital

Working with people in organizations large and small, ranging from the arts and human services to manufacturing, has fueled Mark's fascination with human behavior in the workplace. His diverse experiences share a common pursuit—improving work-life and organizational performance by leveraging human talent, perspective, and motivation. Mark's approach, a unique blending of continuous improvement and organizational development methodologies, has been recognized in forums sponsored by the Manufacturers Alliance for Productivity Improvement, Michigan State University, and others.

Mark holds a masters degree in business administration and is currently pursuing a doctoral degree in organizational psychology.

Hector Velez
Executive Vice President
HireStrategy

Hector Velez, a recognized thought leader in the human capital field, is Executive Vice President of HireStrategy, an *Inc.* 500 firm that provides integrated staffing solutions to organizations in the technology, media, financial services, public, and nonprofit sectors. His role is to design and execute winning strategies in business development, sales, branding, technology, and customer delight. Hector is President of the HR Leadership Forum. He also serves on the board of directors of The SkillSource Group and The Northern Virginia Workforce Investment Board.

Stuart H. Weinstein
Senior Managing Consultant
IBM Global Business Services

Dr. Weinstein has 37 years of professional experience in designing, developing, and delivering instructional products for dissemination via the Internet, computer, satellite, videotape, videodisc, radio, broadcast television, CD-ROM, and classroom for military, civilian government, and commercial clients. He specializes in business process reengineering, strategic and tactical communications planning, management and leadership curricula, and change management. Additionally, he serves as a subject matter expert in attracting graduate students to IBM Learning Solutions careers. Dr. Weinstein earned a BA in Mass Communications and a M.Ed. in Education in Instructional Media from the University of Miami. He holds a Ph.D. in Instructional Systems from Florida State University.

Learning Objectives

Complete this book, and you'll know how to:

1) Implement proactive strategies that address the Millennials' need for increased flexibility and work/life balance.
2) Provide Millennials with multidimensional growth opportunities that meet both their and their organizations' intellectual capital needs.
3) Expand workplace fun and social interaction opportunities that motivate Millennials.
4) Address the Millennials' need to make and be recognized for their contributions to their workplaces and society.
5) Establish and sustain effective communication as a shared responsibility of Millennial and manager.
6) Identify those unique generational factors that influence the importance of recognition, reward, and respect as Millennial motivators.
7) Make the most of Millennials' unique learning preferences with technology-mediated learning methods.
8) Employ strategies that provide financial rewards for knowledge and move beyond the traditional concept of the performance appraisal.

Workplace and Management Competencies mapping

For over 30 years, business and industry has utilized competency models to select employees. The trend to use competency-based approaches in education and training, assessment, and development of workers has experienced a more recent emergence within the Employment and Training Administration (ETA), a division of the United States Department of Labor.

The ETA's General Competency Model Framework spans a wide array of competencies from the more basic competencies, such as reading and writing, to more advanced occupation-specific competencies. The Viva-Crisp Series finds its home in what the ETA refers to as the Workplace Competencies and the Management Competencies.

Motivating the Millennial Knowledge Worker covers information vital to mastering the following **Management** competencies:

- Supporting Others
- Motivating & Inspiring

A Note to Instructors

We've tried to make the Viva-Crisp books as useful as possible as classroom training manuals. Here are some of the features we provide for instructors:

- PowerPoint presentations
- Answer keys
- Assessments
- Customization

PowerPoint Presentations

You can download a PowerPoint presentation for this book from our Web site at www.CrispSeries.com.

Answer keys

If an exercise has specific answers, an answer key will be provided in the appendix. (Some exercises ask you to think about your own opinions or situation; these types of exercises will not have answer keys.)

Assessments

For each 50-Minute Series book, we have developed a 35- to 50-item assessment. The assessment for this book is available at www.CrispSeries.com. *Assessments should not be used in any employee-selection process.*

Understanding the Millennial Knowledge Worker

The intended audience of this book is the line manager and human resources professional faced with the responsibility of understanding and motivating the Millennial worker in the "New Economy." This is an economy, described by Anthony Patrick Carnevale in his book *America and the New Economy*, that has central flexible and information-based technologies. This technology raises the potential for higher quality, productivity, customization, convenience, variety, and timeliness. And the Millennial knowledge worker is quickly emerging as a key driver of this New Economy and our national competitiveness.

Recommendations for Using this Book

This book is the result of a collaborative effort between the author, the publisher, and twenty-one contributing experts. Your understanding of the following five building blocks that serve as the framework of this book will enable you to apply motivational strategies for Millennial knowledge workers. The building blocks are as follows:

- **Understand that motivating Millennials is challenging.**

  This book addresses the specific challenge of motivating the fastest growing segment of the workforce—the Millennial knowledge worker. According to the broadest definition of this term, as presented by Cara Spiro in the article "Generation Y in the Workplace" (*Defense AT&L*, Nov-Dec, 2006), this group numbers almost 80 million Americans born between 1977 and 2000, and accounts for approximately 21 percent of the overall workforce. Other researchers narrow the "anchor years" (explained later in this Introduction) to 1981–1999 (Lancaster and Stillman), while other writers reduce the size of the population (Howe and Straus). This book narrows its focus to college-educated Millennial knowledge workers. Understanding and motivating this newest segment of the workforce is now challenging most human resources professionals.

- **A need exists for an immediately usable tool for motivating Millenials.**

  As both an educator and a consultant, I would be the first person to encourage individuals to address the challenge of motivating Millennial knowledge workers by using resources other than this book. Opportunities may exist to hire a generational consultant, reexamine or restructure the human resources management systems (still in some cases a remnant of a post-industrial era), or at the very least, read a more thorough resource on the subject. However, as a realist and practitioner, I often meet individuals just like you who need an immediate and effective strategy to address the challenge of motivating the Millennial knowledge worker. That need has influenced the content and format of this book.

- **A broad continuum of strategic Millennial motivators is desirable.**

  The parts that follow present discussions of several research-based motivational factors, and strategic examples provided by many Contributing Experts. As you probably know, when it comes to motivation, one size does not fit all. Both the line manager and the human resources professional must develop a broad range of Millennial motivators.

- **The organizational experiences of a variety of contributing experts are invaluable.**

  This book is the result of moving the responsibility for generating the contents of the book from a single author to a team of subject matter experts. This methodology benefits the reader/practitioner in several ways. First, the group of carefully assembled Contributing Experts helped shape the contents of the book by their participation in creating, distributing, and collecting information, using a research-based Millennial Motivational Factors Survey. Second, a synthesis of this survey, discussed in the next chapter, with the experts' experiences results in presenting best-of-class Millennial motivators. These examples drive each chapter, with usable resources in the form of checklists, models, surveys, and tested motivational strategies.

- **There is value in surveying the rapidly growing body of Millennial literature.**

  Each part of this book acknowledges the rich body of literature that currently exists. The research efforts of other authors and consultants are employed to support the strategies and tactics presented throughout this book. This approach has enabled the author and Contributing Experts to narrow the focus of this book to application-oriented strategies that specifically address the motivational needs of the Millennial knowledge worker.

Millennials Defined

"Millennial," as most readers are already aware, is the most commonly used term to describe the subjects of this book. As Neil Howe and William Strauss write in their book *Millennials Rising: The Next Generation,* "For decades Americans have been wishing for a youth generation that would quit talking and start doing… The rising generation will introduce itself to the nation and push the nation into a new era." The authors go on to write that "Once this new youth personnel begins to focus on convention, community and civic renewal, America will be on the brink of becoming someplace very new, very 'Millennial' in the fullest sense of the word."

This book will quote authors of other books that describe our Millennials as "Generation Y," "Gen-Y," "Generation Why," "Echo Boomers," "Generation Next," and other labels. However, "Millennials" has clearly emerged as the preferred name.

It may be worthwhile to take a moment to position the Millennials in a multigenerational perspective. As Carolyn A. Martin and Bruce Tulgan write in *Managing Generation Y: Global Citizens Born in the Late Seventies and Early Eighties*, "Demographers have been unable to agree on the new generation's parameters." There are slight differences in the labels used by different researchers and authors to describe generations. But they all agree on one critical fact. There are currently four generations in the workforce, and there are more similarities in classification than differences. The following table shows three relevant examples.

Model One	Model Two	Model Three
Veterans (b. 1922–1943), Silent	Silent, 62+	Traditionalists (1900–1945)
Baby Boomers (b.1943–1960)	Young/Older Boomers, 45–61	Baby Boomers (1946–1964)
Generation X (b. 1960–1980)	Gen-X , 27–44	Generation Xers (1965–1980)
Nexters (Millennials) (b. 1980–)	Millennials under 26	Millennials (1981–1999)

Again, the focus of this book is on college-educated Millennials who are also knowledge workers. As Ron Alsop writes in *The Trophy Kids Grow Up*, "In addition to more frequent and detailed performance assessments, Millennials want companies to nurture their career development. They are clamoring for more coaching, training, and mentoring programs."

Knowledge Workers

Line managers and human resources professionals—many still using antiquated, post-industrial human resource management systems—not only have to learn how to more effectively identify, understand, and motivate the Millennial, but also must recognize and address the comparable challenge of identifying, understanding, and motivating knowledge workers. When you recognize that Millennial knowledge workers constitute an increasingly larger segment of the workforce, you can see why both managers and human resources professionals face an extraordinary management and development challenge.

Knowledge Worker: Definition and Key Characteristics

In *Managing Knowledge Workers*, Frances Horibe defines "knowledge workers" and summarizes the challenge of managing and motivating knowledge workers.

> ***"[A]t its simplest, knowledge workers are people who use their heads more than their hands to produce value. They add value through their ideas, their analyses, their judgment, their syntheses, and their designs. They still use their hands, of course, but it's more likely to be [for] inputting [information] into a computer than lifting a 50-pound sack."***
>
> **–Frances Horibe**

Horibe talks about the knowledge worker as being the driver of the previously described New Economy, "where a flood of information is coming at lightning speed, changing almost everything." The author further states that in this new economy we find ourselves questioning "how we buy, how we sell, what we make, when we make it, what we value, and where we live. Information is the new driver of wealth creation and those who have it (knowledge workers) are the keys to this new way."

Not only will managers and human resources professionals have to learn how to motivate the Millennials (address their internally driven needs, wants, and desires), but they will also have to learn how to address the human resource development and management challenge of a new economy that is increasingly more characterized by a Millennial knowledge workforce.

To help encapsulate the many challenges of managing and motivating knowledge workers, complete the following inventory, which is based on material appearing in Frances Horibe's book, *Managing Knowledge Workers*.

HR Challenges: An Inventory

Review each of the following challenges and indicate if you agree or disagree with the statement. Also, at the end of the inventory, indicate how you address and support these challenges.

Challenge	Agree	Disagree
1. The driver of success in the New Economy is knowledge.	❑	❑
2. Demand for knowledge workers is great and growing.	❑	❑
3. A knowledge worker is one who uses his/her head more than his/her hands to produce value.	❑	❑
4. About 60 percent of jobs are knowledge based. Managing the human dimension of knowledge workers is the most important job a manager has.	❑	❑

As a manager or human resources professional, I address and support these challenges by:

____

____

____

Motivating people, especially the Millennial knowledge worker, requires identifying strategies that address the needs of a particular segment of the workforce. Managers and human resources professionals cannot overlook the distinct motivational needs of each individual. But for the moment, we will look at motivation from the broader perspective of generational personalities.

> ***"[P]rofessionals… [especially knowledge workers] are best motivated by intangible rewards, such as peer recognition, learning opportunities, opportunities for more independence, and so on."***
>
> **– Karl Erik Sveiby, *The New Organizational Wealth***

Emergence of Generational Personalities

The importance of the notion of generational personalities was first introduced in 1991 when William Strauss and Neil Howe published the now classic book *Generations*, which was later followed by *13 Generations*. Since that time, a number of human resources practitioners have applied this concept to the world of work. In its simplest form, for those readers not familiar with the generation concept, the following three-step generational pattern is generally recognized and accepted.

1. Generations are defined as those Americans born in a twenty-year range between two specific "anchor years." For example, the Baby Boomer generation is widely considered to consist of those people born between 1946 and 1964. These are the anchor years. Other researchers suggest 1943 and 1960 as the generational frame of reference for the same group. The concept remains the same—anchor years within a twenty-year range define a generation.
2. Major events in society that occurred in the formative years of those generations contribute to shaping the personality of these age cohorts, which stays with them throughout life.
3. The differences between generations are claimed to be a major diversity factor affecting American business, human resources development, and management systems.

This concept of generational personalities will be shown to be a driver of motivating the Millennial knowledge worker. Employee productivity is the key to success in the New Economy, and the ability to motivate increasingly determines employee performance and retention.

In fact, understanding multigenerational differences in the workplace can mean the difference between economic success or failure. This is a well-documented return-on-investment case and not a mere human resources issue. It has emerged as a critically important business challenge that has resulted in an explosion of "generational" training programs, videos, articles, and books.

Behavioral Challenges of Millennials

The following quotes help demonstrate that motivating the Millennial knowledge worker is increasingly more challenging for the manager and human resources professional. Which of the following four quotes are most relevant to your challenges in motivating the Millennial knowledge worker?

> ***"The Millennials represent the largest, healthiest, and most cared for generation to ever enter the workforce. This also is a generation with very little real work experience."***
>
> **–Mary Crane, "Mentoring Millennials,"** ***Training Magazine***

> ***"They are independent, techno-savvy, entrepreneurial hard workers who thrive on flexibility. They take these qualities to new heights or transform them."***
>
> **–Carolyn A. Martin and Bruce Tulgan,** ***Managing Generation Y***

> ***"Millennial professionals are multi-taskers, have fast minds, are confident, [are] goal oriented, like balance, and have a strong individual spirit."***
>
> **–Lisa Orrell,** ***Millennials Incorporated***

> ***"They are questioning all the rules, all the time-honored institutions, and all the previously unanswered questions—and they are doing it loudly."***
>
> **–Eric Chester,** ***Employing Generation Why?***

If these behavioral challenges suggest that effective managers and human resources professionals must become more like social scientists, career researchers, or psychologists, you may be right. The new reality for those charged with recruiting and managing Millennials revolves around motivating and retaining the Millennial knowledge worker.

Millennials: A Research and Survey Perspective

Graduates of programs in applied behavior sciences understand that behavior is observable, measurable, predictable, and often, we hope, changeable. This Introduction provides a multidimensional perspective on understanding the behavioral challenge of motivating Millennials. This is accomplished by examining current research and demographical Millennial profiles, reviewing Millennial myths and realities, and sampling the research conclusions of an international human resources management consulting firm.

A Research and Demographical Perspective

In her article titled "Boomers, Xers, and Millennials: What They Really Want from Continuing Higher Education," Cathy Sandeen, Dean of Continuing Education and Extension at the University of California-Los Angeles, presents a demographical snapshot of Millennials. She states that "The Millennial generations (born between 1982 and 2003) experience a shift back to a child-centered social context. This time period represented the lowest child-to-parent ratio in American history." Some highlights of her discussion follow, in the format of a behavioral quiz.

DID YOU KNOW?
A MILLENNIAL BEHAVIORAL QUIZ

Identify the five Millennial behavioral characteristics most relevant to your organization. Discuss these challenges with your colleagues, and generate strategies to address the behavioral legacies that Millennials bring to the workplace.

____ 1. Concern with quality of education emerged, and standardized test scores began to increase.

____ 2. Parents of Millennials seemed obsessed with preparing their children for the future.

____ 3. Millennial children began building their résumés in preschool, attending the best schools and participating in a plethora of extra-curricular activities.

____ 4. They are a pressured and achieving generation.

CONTINUED

CONTINUED

____ 5. Millennials are trusting of their parents and other authority figures.

____ 6. Millennials are team-oriented, confident, and optimistic.

____ 7. They grew up with computers; they experienced the rapid adoption of the Internet, cell phones, and other mobile devices.

____ 8. They are a highly networked, connected generation and tend to be completely immersed in technology.

____ 9. Millennials are graduating from college and entering graduate school.

____ 10. They tend to be very career oriented and expect rapid advancement and perks.

____ 11. Millennials appreciate feedback, having been graded, evaluated, and ranked throughout their lives.

____ 12. Because of their skill at multitasking, Millennials are likely to want to build parallel careers, not focusing on one job or profession at the exclusion of another.

____ 13. Multitasking may ultimately take the form of continuous job-changing for Millennials.

____ 14. Because of their community orientation, they tend to appreciate mission-driven organizations.

____ 15. They are motivated by helping others, improving the environment, and making the world a better place.

Millennial Myths and Realities

Robert Half International, one of the world's first and largest specialized staffing firms, and Yahoo! HotJobs present still another study of Millennials, entitled *What Millennial Workers Want: How to Attract and Retain Gen Y Employees*. The following information was based on a survey of 1,007 people between the ages of 21–28 who are employed full-time or part-time and have college degrees or are attending college. This survey revealed five Millennial myths and facts. The following quote from the study sets the stage for them.

> ***"In reality, our survey results point to an ambitious, highly motivated generation that shares many of the same concerns as their predecessors. In fact, the survey respondents appear more attuned to issues such as saving for retirement, having good health care benefits, and balancing work and personal obligations than might be expected of those who are relatively new to the workforce. Much of this may be due to the fact that they've witnessed significant uncertainty in their lifetimes, making security and stability increasingly attractive, both in their personal lives and on the job."***
>
> ***What Millennial Workers Want: How to Attract and Retain Gen Y Employees***

TEST YOUR ASSUMPTIONS

Read and discuss each of the following five Millennial myths with your fellow managers and human resources professionals before reviewing the corresponding facts.

Myth One: Generation Y (Millennials) lives in the moment and would rather play than work.

Myth Two: Generation Y expects instant gratification.

Myth Three: This generation slacks off at work to take care of personal matters.

Myth Four: Generation Y workers can't take direction.

Myth Five: Generation Y employees have a sense of entitlement.

After discussing each of the above myths with your colleagues, reconcile your answers with the facts.

Fact One: Millennials are most concerned about supporting themselves and their families, saving enough money, finding and keeping a job, and having career satisfaction.

Fact Two: They're focused on the future and worried about funding their retirement.

Fact Three: Seventy-three percent worry about balancing professional and personal obligations.

Fact Four: They want frequent communication with their bosses.

Fact Five: They expect to pay their dues in different ways.

At *www.rhi.com*, you can read the entire article that these five "Millennial Myths and Facts" were selected from; it might provide additional insights into motivating the Millennial knowledge worker.

Sharing Responsibility for Motivating the Millennial Knowledge Worker

Managers and human resources professionals face the challenge of reconciling the expectations of employee and employer. As one component of an employment contract, they must not overlook the importance of the physical, psychological, and social aspects of the environment.

The Three E's: Employee, Employer, and Environment

Jeffrey Zaslow's article "The Most Praised Generation Goes to Work," which appeared in *The Wall Street Journal* (April 20, 2007), discusses three specific challenges of dealing with "the Über-stroked kids reaching adulthood." He makes two important statements:

> ***"Childhood in recent decades has been defined by stroking—by parents who see their job as building self-esteem, by soccer coaches who give every player a trophy, by schools that used to name one student of the month and these days name 40."***

> ***"Now, as the greatest generation grows up, the culture of praise is reaching deeply into the adult world. Bosses, professors, and mates are feeling the need to lavish praise on young adults, particularly twenty-somethings, or see them wither under an unfamiliar compliment deficit."***

Zaslow outlines three employer/employee concerns relevant to motivating the Millennial knowledge worker:

1. Praise inflation
2. Modern pressures
3. No more red pens

The following Agree/Disagree inventory, based on his article, summarizes these concepts and provides a tool you can use with your colleagues to assess the impact of these behaviors on motivating and managing Millennials.

AN INVENTORY FOR MILLENNIAL MANAGERS

Indicate whether you agree (A) or disagree (D) with each of the following motivational factors, and discuss these items with your colleagues.

Praise Inflation	A	D
1. Employers say the praise culture can help them with job retention.	❑	❑
2. People's positive traits can be exaggerated until the words feel meaningless.	❑	❑
3. It's important to make at least five positive statements for each negative one.	❑	❑
4. Many managers are joining "America's excessive praise parade" to hold onto young workers.	❑	❑
5. Workers under 40 require more stroking and rewards and want more constant feedback.	❑	❑
Modern Pressures	**A**	**D**
1. Heightened pressure to perform in today's demanding firms has created a culture where you have to give instant feedback or you will fail.	❑	❑
2. Gen Y-ers don't just say they want feedback. They are also saying they require it.	❑	❑
3. One company encourages managers to start every meeting with informal recognition.	❑	❑
4. Managers need to get a sense of how Millennials like to be praised—in public or one-on-one in the office.	❑	❑
5. Organizations should be encouraged to develop formal mechanisms. One is called "S.A.Y. It" cards: "someone appreciates you."	❑	❑

CONTINUED

CONTINUED

No More Red Pens	A	D
1. Some young adults are consciously calibrating their dependence on praise—they are on the border of the Millennial generation that requires over-praise and a thirtysomething generation that is less addicted to praise.	❑	❑
2. University professors have attended seminars to learn techniques of supportive criticism. You need to throw away your red pens to avoid intimidating students.	❑	❑
3. When people are lousy, they need to be told that. Ego-stroking may feel good, but it doesn't lead to happiness.	❑	❑
4. We need to declare a moratorium on meaningless and baseless praise that often begins in nursery school. "I am special, look at me."	❑	❑
5. Organizations should follow the Scooter Stores model and hire "celebration assistants," charged with throwing confetti, filling balloons, and showing up at employees' desks to offer high-fives.	❑	❑

The Employer's Perspective: New Work Rules for Millennials

Rob McGovern, CEO of Jobfox, brings a unique employer perspective to the challenge of motivating Millennials. He has worked for several well-known companies, including Hewlett-Packard, Disney, and IBM. He also founded and later sold his company, CareerBuilder. At the age of 30, he wrote the book *Bring Your "A" Game: The 10 Career Secrets of High Achievers*, targeted at Gen X and Gen Y people. From this multidimensional perspective, he wrote what has come to be a Millennial mantra: "Companies must learn to hire, appreciate, and motivate younger workers, or they will perish."

An Employer's Portrait of Millennials

Rob McGovern writes that Generation Y is the most educated and most technologically savvy generation ever. Yet companies continue to have biases against younger workers. In a Jobfox poll of more than 200 recruiters, 63 percent rated Baby Boomers as "greater" performers in their organizations. This compares to 58 percent who rated Gen X as greater performers, 20 percent for Gen Y, and 25 percent for our older workers, the Traditionalists.

In short, Rob McGovern states that "companies don't think highly of Gen-Y (or older workers). I think it's because companies don't understand them. But those that do will gain a competitive advantage. Just as there were workplace changes made to accommodate Baby Boomers and Gen-Xers, I foresee changes ahead as Gen-Y grows in the workplace."

Having interviewed hundreds of younger workers for *Bring Your "A" Game*, Rob McGovern learned a few things about Generation Y:

1. **They crave stability.**

   The Gen Y world is full of instability. Ask them about the world and they might talk about hurricanes, tsunamis, 9/11, Code Orange alerts, three wars, and AIDS. They live in a world with a constant "News Alert" crawling at the bottom of their TV monitors. They watched their parents turn the word "downsized" into a verb. With this set of experiences as a frame of reference, Gen Y would like to think of a company as a refuge. If we can meet their other needs, which I will discuss next, I think we'll see tenure begin to rise again in the decades ahead.

2. **They want balance.**

   Younger workers play for different rewards. With Baby Boomers, all you had to do was wave $10,000 more and a promotion in front of them and they were on their way. Gen Y doesn't want this. Gen Y, instead, wants a little balance to go with the American dream. Give flexible hours. These workers just don't understand the rigidity of the world that the Baby Boomers have created. "Why can't I work 12 hours a day, three days a week? Why does it have to be your way?"

3. **They want to take charge.**

   Gen Y doesn't want to be a junior anything. This is the generation that looked out the car window past the "Baby on Board" sign. This is a generation with helicopter parents who told them every day that they are "special and entitled to speak up to make something of themselves." This is a generation that believes everyone deserves a trophy, win or lose. So, here comes a big corporation. What do we do? We put them in a sea of look-alike cubicles and tell them to learn the ropes if they want to make something of themselves.

   They want to make a contribution on the first day. As companies, we need to do a better job of addressing their sense of contribution. Gen Y will not be satisfied working inside the machine. We need to work with them to help them see how their actions are connected to organizational goals.

> ***"If we went into a time machine today and went forward in time, I would not be surprised to see companies with three-day work weeks, addressing new Gen-X/Gen-Y learning styles. It's going to happen. Especially as younger workers inherit leadership roles, giving them a place where they feel like they belong."***
>
> **–Rob McGovern, "Attracting and Retaining Young Professionals"**

The Millennial Workers' Environment

Neil Sawyer introduces the last of the "Three E's"—Environment. The company that he has had experience with earned a place on the "Best Places to Work for" list published by *Publishers Executive Magazine*. The organization, a leading publisher in Washington, D.C., is referred to as "Leading Publisher" in this Introduction. The company's Web site states that "The company hires professionals who are smart, competitive, and fast." Sawyer presents the following case for the appropriate Millennial environment. How does your organization meet these needs?

The Leading Publisher's employee population has a large portion of young employees (between 22 and 33 years old). These employees fill a wide range of job functions, including, but not limited to, graphic artists, print and online editors, Web designers, IT professionals, and administrative support personnel.

Three Unique Environmental Factors: The Leading Publisher prides itself on its unique corporate culture. While embodying many of the mainstream philosophies, it seeks to include younger employees and promote a workplace that is not stereotypical. Three aspects show this deviation from the "corporate American" feel.

1. **The architecture and workspaces of the Leading Publisher's offices:**

   All offices of the Leading Publisher are designed and decorated with respect given to "what would an energetic, style-conscious, young employee want to see in his/her workplace?" The CEO's personal art collection graces the hallways on three floors of the corporate headquarters, and the furniture is hand-picked for its trend-setting style.

2. **The relaxed dress code at the Leading Publisher:**

   Employees are told from their first day on the job that there is no dress code. The philosophy is that we are adults who can make our own choices regarding what is appropriate attire. While some employees prefer to wear shorts and flip-flops during the summer months, others opt for business casual, and to date, no employee has ever needed to be counseled on their attire choices.

3. **The open-door policy of the CEO:**

   Employees are told during the orientation luncheon with the CEO that if they ever have a question or concern about the company or its practices, they may come see him personally. Younger employees routinely take him up on his offer. The CEO doesn't just listen to the concerns of these employees; he acts on them. Human Resources has in the past been tasked to do research and suggest alternative ways of conducting aspects of the business, based on these informal conversations with staff.

There is no magic formula for creating an effective Millennial culture for each organization. The environment is influenced by the company's products and services. However, the three previously outlined environmental factors clearly enhanced the Millennial culture of the Leading Publisher in Washington, D.C.

Millennial Motivational Issues

The goal of the author and Contributing Experts has been to create an immediately usable resource that identifies those specific Millennial motivators, and provides strategies and tactics to address them.

A variety of checklists, inventories, and assessments are presented throughout the book. These are helpful resources for immediate application of strategies and are designed to achieve the following objectives:

- **Acknowledge broader issues related to motivating Millenials.** While the focus of this book is specifically on motivating Millennial knowledge workers, the reader/practitioner should also be aware of broader human resource management issues that also affect Millennials.
- **Present multiple perspectives on Millennials.** Effectively motivating Millennials requires an understanding of how different stakeholders view the Millennial. With this in mind, four Contributing Experts present their perspective on Millennials; the experts are a Millennial, a recruiter, a human resource manager, and a workforce consultant.
- **Explain the research-based methodology that generated sixteen Millennial motivators.** Through the use of research and survey methodologies, and the active involvement of the twenty-one Contributing Experts featured in this book, sixteen Millennial motivators were identified. These motivators drive the following eight parts of the book.

Motivating Millennials

As we seek to understand Millennial motivational issues, it's important that we examine several global workforce issues that have dramatically changed the way in which organizations manage their human capital.

The following list of four broad Millennial motivational issues will provide you with an opportunity to assess and rank the issues that affect your organization. The checklist may also serve as a discussion resource for various business units and workgroups.

FOUR MILLENNIAL MOTIVATIONAL ISSUES

Review each of the following items and rank the importance of each one, using a scale of 1–5 (with 5 the highest). Discuss these items with your business unit and/or workgroup.

____ 1. **The emergence of a global economy has created a workforce crisis.** The current concern for recruiting, retaining, and motivating Millennials is rooted in a much broader issue—the emergence of a highly competitive global workforce.

Thomas Friedman reinforces this reality in *The World is Flat* by stating, "Cheap ubiquitous telecommunication has finally obliterated all impediments to international competition," and "American workers should be prepared to create value with leadership and sell personality."

The challenge is how to keep workers engaged and loyal to your firm.

____ 2. **Learning is not only a Millennial motivator, but also a link that is connected to business strategies.** Peter M. Senge's 1990 book, *The Fifth Discipline: The Art and Practice of the Learning Organization,* formalized the concept that "In the long run, the only sustainable source of competitive advantage is your organization's ability to learn faster than its competition."

An organization that promotes learning and then "stands ready to quickly capitalize on that information" will be the type of organization that will move forward successfully into the next decade (Michael J. Marquardt, *Building Learning Organizations*).

Providing Millennials with career development opportunities through continuous learning is not only a motivator for them, but also has a critical return-on-investment factor.

Given the increasing pressures of global demographic shifts, economic challenges, and the complexity of retaining talent, more companies are turning to learning and development as a way to improve performance, improve motivation, develop required skills, and sustain productivity.

CONTINUED

CONTINUED

____ 3. **Generational issues are business issues.** Today's employers are faced with managing a multigenerational workforce.

Carolyn A. Martin, Ph.D., and Bruce Tulgan address this issue at the beginning of their book *Managing the Generation Mix: From Collision to Collaboration,* stating:

- Generational problems are important reflections of critical business issues facing organizations that are transitioning from a workplace of the past to that of the future.
- Your challenge as a manager of a workplace mix of four generations (also called Gen Mix) is to steer your multi-generation team members off the rigid course of "business as usual" into an open field of innovation, productivity, and learning.
- Many organizations have finally figured out how to recruit young talent, only to watch them drive down a collision course with seasoned employees over issues of work ethics, respect for authority, dress code, and every work arrangement imaginable.

____ 4. **Technology and demographics are on a collision course.** Not only is there a challenge in managing a mix of four generations in the workforce, but now there is the additional challenge of managing across the technology gap.

In his book *Generation Blend: Managing Across the Technology Age Gap*, Rob Salkowitz presents the following points to reinforce the importance of this challenge:

- Generational attitudes toward technology affect issues as diverse as recruitment and retention, employee training, management decision making, collaboration, knowledge sharing, work/life balance, and ordinary work habits.
- Organizations are scrambling to unlock the talents of a multigenerational workforce in a connected world.
- The retirement of the Baby Boomers, the arrival of the Millennials, and the impact of Web 2.0 create unprecedented complexity for employers and workers in the 2010s and beyond.

The issues and challenges are to identify what initiatives can be launched to bridge the divide in work styles and technological skills that separates veterans from newcomers to the workforce.

Generational Strategies vs. Workforce Talent Management

There's no doubt that the concept of a generational approach to human resource management is an improvement over the more traditional one-size-fits all HRM system of recruiting, selecting, managing, motivating, developing, and retaining employees. However, a more sophisticated and effective strategy should also be considered. Rick Humphress, a Contributing Expert for this book, makes the case for moving beyond a simple generational strategy to employing a more comprehensive four-stage strategy for managing workforce talent.

The Four-stage Talent Management Strategy

Rick Humphress, Public Sector HCM Specialist
Oracle Corporation

Public- and private-sector organizations use talent management practices to increase the productivity and reduce the costs associated with the workforce. Typical talent management practices include succession and career planning, strategic staffing, pay for performance, training, and performance management. These talent management practices are evolving through four stages as they are applied to the workforce.

First, organizations apply talent management practices uniformly through the employee population without regard to any differences or distinctions. This one-size-fits-all approach is easy to implement, administer, and maintain. However, it is difficult to adapt to changing conditions and it generates high employee turnover.

Next, organizations apply talent management practices differently based on sociological differences between generations—Traditionalists, Baby Boomers, Generation X, or Gen Y (Millennials). Although it's an improvement over the homogeneous approach, the generational approach is still rather broad since it divides 150 million workers into just four categories. Talent management practices are still blunt instruments without any individual precision.

Next, organizations apply talent management practices differently based on specific worker temperaments or types (e.g., the Myers-Briggs Type Indicator, or MBTI). This approach divides the worker population into several categories (sixteen in the case of MBTI) to which talent management practices can be adapted.

Finally, at the finest level of granularity, talent management practices can be precisely tailored to meet the needs of each individual. A talent-management rules engine can interact with each individual employee profile to generate a deeply personalized and unique performance improvement plan for each person.

The driving force behind progressing through these four stages of talent management deployment is computer automation. Manual systems promote homogeneous practices because it is just too difficult to create multiple talent management approaches. Achieving deeply personalized talent management, however, takes more than software and hardware.

First, the talent management rules must be established. Second, the employee profiles must be in a centralized HR database. Third, the various talent management practices must be integrated applications and not isolated information silos. Finally, the organization must be willing to make a commitment to a holistic view of HR as a complex system that can be continuously improved.

Four Portraits of Millennials

Here, we introduce four perspectives on Millennials: those of a Millennial, a recruiter, a human resources manager, and a workforce consultant. As you read each of the following four portraits, consider jotting down your thoughts, observations, and lessons learned on the worksheet that follows the last perspective.

A Millennial's Self-Portrait

Erin Nicole Gordon
Accenture

Raised by the Baby Boomers, we emerge on the scene as "high maintenance" with our laptops and continual texting. We are "Millennials"—often characterized as demanding, inflexible, inexperienced, gregarious, and even loud. However, these descriptions don't fit all Millennials. In contrast to the typical Millennial profile, the Millennial knowledge worker, with which I identify, represents a high-performing, task-oriented group with a high capacity to learn and grow.

In portraying the Millennial knowledge worker, I suggest a subset of adjectives introducing thoughtful contradictions to stereotypes and highlighting our potential. These adjectives set the stage for factors motivating the Millennial knowledge worker and describe how I personally identify with the group addressed in this book. Attributes revealing how best to strategically motivate the Millennial knowledge worker will be discussed in the snapshot to follow. These characteristics include: independent or do-it-yourself (DIY), engaged, ambitious, innovative, and compassionate. Each attribute acknowledged and thoughtfully considered will serve to realize the possibilities of a Millennial knowledge worker.

Flexibility and Work/Life Balance. As an independent worker, I value the flexibility to work where and when best fits my schedule. Moreover, I prefer to work when maximum levels of productivity are possible, and that certainly does not conform to the 8 a.m.–5 p.m. norm of conducting business. The flexibility component in scheduling work also offers me the authority to choose my priorities, whether work or activities beyond my career. By providing flexibility, my employer addresses the factor of work-life balance, another quality of work I value highly. Like most Millennial knowledge workers, I pursue life outside of work and dedicate much of my time to interests outside my career. While work is a priority, I prefer a balance and the freedom to seek that balance. As I am given the flexibility to work independently, I become increasingly more productive and am more likely to collaborate with others given the new time created by flexible parameters.

Recognition. When graduates seek employment after college, common assumptions often set expectations. Whether the assumption results from teaching, observation of parents' experiences, or mere perceptions, I recall most classmates, myself included, acknowledging "serving time" in our first positions as a requirement. This meant succumbing to the requests of an employer in return for the willingness to meet personal needs for a short period of time, namely, earning the respect needed to work independently.

A second assumption makes clear why numerous Millennial knowledge workers expect respect quickly. We assume that our first job's purpose is only to prepare us for the next career move, which should occur in three years at most. We anticipate moving on almost immediately, gaining the mutual trust and respect necessary to succeed. The do-it-yourself, independent nature of the Millennial knowledge worker creates needs for employment to be flexible, allowing the option to seek an appropriate work/life balance if expectations for productivity are well-defined from the beginning.

Multidimensional Millennial Growth Opportunities. Recognizing independence by offering flexibility and work/life balance is essential to motivating the knowledge worker. Further still, a focus upon the engaged, ambitious attitude of this group is at the heart of motivating Millennials and retaining high-quality resources. Growth opportunities coupled with ways to actively contribute fuel the fire of ambition in many Millennials. College recruitment efforts with my current employer demonstrate the continual demand for growth opportunities in coming generations; candidates often request models for career development or program overviews to indicate how career advancement may be achieved. I interviewed with a variety of employers, inquired about developmental opportunities, and turned away all employment not exhibiting a clear path for advancement with fast-paced progression.

The Millennial knowledge worker seeks multidimensional growth opportunities that may be found through mentorship, executive/client interaction, or simply rich, informal relationships. From a team perspective, group projects to gain exposure or introduce challenges with problem-solving elements present engaging activities with added social benefit. Other developmental prospects include networking engagements, community involvement, and nonprofit work. Any opportunity allowing leadership or service involvement typically wins the interest of a Millennial. Because contribution is no longer defined as merely increasing profit, these diverse growth opportunities allow for both development and uniquely individual ways to contribute in an organization.

Purpose, Contribution, and Challenging Work. Like many Millennial knowledge workers, I seek a sense of purpose in my career; knowing that I make an identified difference in my work is a significant reward. In the past, growth was measured by promotions or titles, but recognition for contributions no longer means monetary gains or a corner office. I personally find more motivation in being extended the opportunity to give back to the community than in increased pay.

The ability to give back to the community in some way while working will ultimately make most menial tasks worthwhile to a Millennial knowledge worker because the societal contribution seems to matter more in the long run than any slight promotion received to advance a career.

Fun and Social Interaction. As already implied, there is an element of compassion that characterizes the Millennial knowledge worker. This compassion often combines with fun and social interaction, all of which motivate high-performing workers. Whereas there once existed clearly defined times for work and play, these distinctions fade for a Millennial. We work and play simultaneously, just as we choose when and where we do so. Similarly, we find no differentiation between work and community service. As evidenced by the many corporate initiatives and missions that now include developmental and service-oriented relationships (working and being involved all at once), there is a clear effort to engage the cause-oriented Millennial knowledge worker like myself. We use these opportunities to exercise our creativity and leverage our innovative, tech-savvy capabilities to maximize our work around the clock. We have no bounds and only need continual support to continually deliver high performance.

As I observe various projects and find a myriad of twenty-somethings tucked into cubicles, I see that this firm "gets" the Millennial knowledge worker. Kudos to corporate efforts—we must recognize that our employers are aware and willing to work with these and all differentiating attributes we bring to the table in order to keep us motivated. We possess the potential to sustain competitive advantages sought in the corporate setting—just ensure that we do not lose wireless access!

A Millennial Recruiter's Perspective

Nicole Hardin
HireStrategy, Inc.

Over the past several decades, the relationship between employer and employee has been evolving, and with the overwhelming number of Millennials joining the workforce, it is likely that we will see a new paradigm created. The expectations of the Millennial worker are distinctly different from those of their older counterparts already in the workforce. Key criteria that Millennials are using to decide where they will be working include the following:

- **They want to work with their friends.** This generation is evaluating their future employers by how they envision their relationships with co-workers. It is a given that Millennials expect to work with people who are as bright, capable, and driven as they are. In addition, however, they expect that they will make social connections, to some degree, with their team members.
- **They expect a coach/mentor, not a boss.** They have been coached their whole lives and they expect nothing different from their direct manager. It is important to keep in mind that many Millennials view their parents as friends and will expect the same kind of mentor relationship from their boss.

- **They are passionate about developing, evolving, and being rewarded.** This is the generation that seeks instant gratification, and they want an environment where they are reminded (constantly) that their work matters and they are making a difference. The good news is, they aren't as driven by jumps in compensation or meaningless promotions. Their focus is much more on learning new skills and knowing that their work is making a real impact.
- **They want to be part of something "bigger than themselves."** This may be one of the most socially aware generations ever. Millennials will be partial to a company that has a mission that benefits society. The good news is that they are excellent team players, and when they feel like part of a mission, this skill is further enhanced.
- **They, more than any other generation in the past, have a very clear picture of what they want, and they feel entitled to it now.** They see no reason to pay their dues or work somewhere they don't like in order to gain valuable experience. They want good experience in a good environment and are unlikely to make many compromises.
- **Their parents will be integral in their decisions about where they work.** Millennials have always looked to their parents as partners in life decisions, and this decision is no different.

As a result, many companies have responded to these Millennial requirements with the following strategies:

- **Most companies have done a lot of work to develop their corporate cultures.** They have recognized that throwing a ping-pong table in the break room isn't, in itself, a culture, and they have invested time and resources into making it a real part of the organization. Furthermore, most companies have become much better at marketing their cultures to prospective employees. In the past, it was enough to say "we are a great place to work." Companies are now demonstrating why they are a great place to work.
- **Companies have worked to create smaller steps in career paths** to keep employees engaged and feeling rewarded more regularly.
- **We have seen a rise in corporate events** (usually smaller, informal gatherings) to promote the social component that this generation craves.
- **Companies have put a lot more emphasis on their recruiting processes.** This is no longer just a focus for HR. Companies are investing time and training with not only their managers but also their team leads and anyone who is involved in the interview process. There has been a shift to ensure that the interview not only evaluates the candidate's skills but also sells the candidates on investing their talents in this organization.

Those strategies are a good start, but there are some additional steps that can bridge the Millennial/employer gap even further. For example:

- **The key to securing and retaining the Millennial generation is their manager.** They need to have a manager who is open to constant communication and regular praise. They want to constantly be gaining new responsibilities and taking on more and more meaningful work. They need a manager who has bought into "them," not just "the work they do." Millennials need to believe that their manager has a strong commitment to their development, and need to see their manager demonstrate this on a daily basis through mentorship.
- **Companies need to get better at demonstrating how what they do affects society and showing that they are socially conscious.**
- **It would behoove many companies to start working on a plan for how they can influence the parents in the recruiting process.**
- **The more clearly companies can lay out a development program, the more likely a Millennial will be to make a commitment to the organization.** The plan doesn't have to show all upward mobility. It's important to remember that this generation is accustomed to constant motion, so put some ability for them to move horizontally into their development plan. They want to learn and be challenged, and you can do that without making them managers.

Three Recurring Themes

Shaara Roman, HR Director
CGI Federal

In my dealings with Millennials as an HR executive, I have experienced three recurring themes, and offer the following advice to managers of Gen Y employees:

1. **Provide a learning environment.** Millennials want an environment in which they can constantly learn and be mentored. They want to have access to information when they need it, and they want training accessible 24/7. They want opportunities to explore different roles and career paths, and they want an organization that will allow them to advance in their career.

   Provide a clear career path: Manage the employee's impatience to get to the next level by being concrete and deliberate in creating a path to get there. Share your expectations of specific behaviors, experiences, or deliverables that are needed before the employee can get to the next level.

   Be supportive of your employees, engage in dialogue, and be supportive of their decisions and choices. Show that you will actively work with an employee and champion his choice for career growth, even if it is not with your team. Provide direct and constructive feedback, but be open to receiving feedback yourself.

2. **Provide a social environment.** Our Gen Y employees repeatedly cite our company-funded social club as a benefit they value greatly. It also gives them the sense that the organization is committed to meeting their needs. In addition to having formal opportunities to socialize with co-workers, Millennials want to know that they are working with people who could be friends. They want to be able to relax and go to happy hours, sporting events, and so on with their work colleagues.

   Chill a little. As a manager, try to provide an environment that is friendly and relaxed. Every now and then, when possible, build in some downtime, whether it's in a team meeting once a quarter or a happy hour. Celebrate birthdays and service anniversaries. Allow opportunities for team members to recognize each other. On occasion, grab a coffee with your employee or walk to the sandwich store together.

3. **Provide a flexible environment.** I envy Millennials because they have a life! Gen Y-ers are vocal about expressing their thoughts—which are really not that much different from ours. They are not clock-watchers, and they are de-motivated by having to adhere to what may seem like an arbitrary schedule. While work is not the number-one priority, Millennials will work hard to accomplish what needs to be done.

   Manage by outcomes. I would suggest revisiting the notion of hard and fast start and end times for the work day. Instead, pick "core hours," such as 10 a.m. to 3 p.m., when everyone is expected to be in the office. The most effective way to manage Millennials in a professional setting is to provide a deliverable and a deadline. How and when the work gets done is really up to the individual. The individual will almost always come through. The flexibility and autonomy to set their schedule makes Millennials feel respected and valued for their contributions. I find that if you give a little, you will get a lot in return.

Portrait of a Millennial

Kris T. Jensen, Vice President, Corporate Services
Wisdom Worker Solutions

As each generation enters the workforce, its behaviors are shaped by the realities currently evident in the world. While some realities may be held in common, Millennials who came of age in the 1990s will have experienced slightly different world realities than those who just started turning 16 in 2009. With that in mind, consider the following:

- **A skill package versus a profession**

  Millennials recognize that versatility both reinforces their value to their current employer and increases their marketability to any organization. Consequently, rather than being categorized by a profession or an industry, they focus on obtaining a comprehensive set of skills that employers identify as critical to success in the workplace.

Millennials are often self-confident, resourceful, collegial, open, expressive, and direct. However, they will need development in interpersonal skills, basic English writing, coping skills, and critical thinking skills.

- **A global tribe**

Shifting socio-economic factors worldwide have given Millennials the opportunity to grow, learn, and live with more diverse people. This openness to diversity has also contributed to the redefinition of the nuclear family. Parents, who have highly active roles in Millennial lives, have solicited their input on a variety of family decisions, leading Millennials to expect to be consulted in the workplace and to exercise their personal choice. Concerns about their personal safety in schools, organizations, and in public have led some sociologists to acknowledge that Millennials may have a polarized view of the world. (Studies conducted by the Center for Creative Leadership have identified few behavioral differences among generations from country to country.)

- **Virtually real**

Millennials have been raised in the virtual world. Documenting the most intimate details of their lives in videos, in photos, and on social networking Web pages, they have a broader sense of their virtual reality, which redefines privacy. This 24/7 lifestyle has some believing that while Millennials have greater work/life balance, they might need to be "unplugged" from time to time to forestall burnout and related health issues. Immersion in technology should not be confused with competence, as not all Millennials are technically adept to the same degree. Most, however, have an understanding of how technology has the "power to personalize." Those who work diligently to protect those of us surfing in the virtual world suggest that Millennials may be naïve and too trusting of those they find online.

- **A growing conscience**

Ultimately Millennials will reach and overtake the footprint of the Baby Boomers. As they grow into their size, there is a corresponding social awareness rising, much as the Boomers heralded a period of great social change. Millennials recognize the world realities they may be inheriting, including a burgeoning federal debt, significant unemployment, and an impaired planet. Generational scholars state that every fourth generation represents a period in which society redefines its nature and purpose. Protected as children, Millennials will likely return to being institutionally driven with a trust in authority, making them powerful elders that will provoke the conscientious change typically instigated by a fourth generation.

PORTRAITS OF A MILLENNIAL: LESSONS LEARNED

Now that you have reviewed the four Millennial portraits, identify the lessons gleaned from each perspective.

Lessons learned from the Millennial's perspective:

____

____

____

____

Lessons learned from the Millennial recruiter's perspective:

____

____

____

____

Lessons learned from the human resources manager:

____

____

____

____

Lessons learned from the Millennial-workforce consultant:

____

____

____

____

Summary

This introduction had three main objectives: first, to acknowledge issues related to motivating Millennials; second, to present four perspectives of Millennials; and third, to explain the research-based methodology that produced the sixteen Millennial motivators that appear in this book:

- Flexibility and work/life balance
- Multidimensional Millennial growth opportunities
- Fun and social interaction
- Purpose, contribution, and challenging work
- Establishing and sustaining excellent communications
- The three R's: recognition, respect, and rewards
- Learning, training, and technology
- Pay for performance

As you begin to use this book as a resource to motivate your Millennial knowledge workers, you can do so sequentially or by selecting those sections most relevant to your immediate needs.

PART 1

Flexibility and Work/Life Balance

> *"Kids in their twenties are all about figuring out how to find balance and not being stuck in a career path that shoots straight to the top. What is more important is that they do something that is valuable and meaningful."*
>
> *–New Options, New Talent: The Government Guide to the Flexible Workforce*

In this part:

- Getting Started
- Flexibility and Work/Life Balance: Not New Concepts
- Perspectives on Flexibility and Work/Life Balance
- Proactive Strategies Supporting Flexibility and Work/Life Balance
- Flexibility and Work/Life Balance: Examples

Getting Started

Each of the eight parts of this book focuses on one or more "Millennial motivators." These were identified, as described in the Introduction, through the use of research and survey methodologies and the active involvement of the twenty-one Contributing Experts featured in this book. Sixteen Millennial motivational factors were identified and are now presented.

It was not surprising that flexibility emerged at the top of the list in the Motivational Factors Survey, with over 80 percent of the respondents ranking it as the most important motivator. Work/life balance also made it to the top-ten list. As the research and writing process progressed, it became apparent that flexibility and work/life balance are interdependent factors in meeting the motivational needs of Millennial knowledge workers. Part 1 builds on this conclusion by addressing the following four objectives:

- Understanding that flexibility and work/life balance are not new concepts
- Appreciating that the current workforce crisis is driving the need for flexible work arrangements
- Recognizing the need to take a closer look at Millennials and their need for increased flexibility and work/life balance
- Implementing proactive strategies in support of flexibility and work/life balance

Flexibility and Work/Life Balance: Not New Concepts

Although flexibility and work/life balance have emerged as important motivational factors for Millennial knowledge workers, these concepts are certainly not new to the workplace or workforce. Human resource managers, researchers, and employers have addressed this issue, as the following brief discussion summarizes.

Work/Life Balance

The concept of work/life balance is not new. During past decades, both here in the United States and in other countries, employees have been working harder and working longer hours, and as the research indicates, often feel that they don't have enough time for their spouses, their children, and themselves. What is unique, according to Erica D. Chick, writing in *Fundamentals of Work-Life Balance*, "is that the role of work itself has changed from a matter of survival to a matter of personal satisfaction. People often work more to achieve success in their personal lives."

While implementing a plan for work/life balance has been a "desirable" for the past generation, it is now a well-documented "essential" for Millennial knowledge workers. They ask themselves and their employers, "How do I balance competing demands to ensure that I am spending my time most effectively in areas that are of value to me?" Later in this part, recommendations will be made to help Millennials address this concern.

Flexibility

The motivational factor of flexibility is not an exclusively Millennial issue. It is, in the broadest sense, part of an employee-employer equation that has the potential to satisfy the needs and suit the lifestyles of each generation in the workplace. However, as with work/life balance, for the Millennial knowledge worker, flexibility is not merely desirable, but rather is essential.

According to Ken Dychtwald, Tamara J. Erickson, and Robert Morison, authors of *Workforce Crisis: How to Beat the Coming Shortage of Skills and Talent,* three components of flexibility are required to create a customized "employment deal." These components are flexible work arrangements, flexible learning opportunities, and flexible compensation and benefits. The following short exercise, based on material selected from their book, is presented in the form of an inventory to further explore the concept of flexibility.

THE FLEXIBLE EMPLOYMENT DEAL

Identify which of the following flexibility components characterize your organization's or business unit's current strengths, and identify any areas that require further development.

1. **Flexible work arrangements.** Does your organization:

   - ❑ Customize work schedules, locations, and formats to engender productivity and loyalty?
   - ❑ Enable teleworkers and other flex workers to stay connected with the organization, both socially and electronically?

2. **Flexible learning opportunities.** Does your organization:

   - ❑ Adopt multiple learning methods to meet the needs of diverse learners?
   - ❑ Use learning experiences to bring groups together?
   - ❑ Leverage the learning potential and efficiency of information technology?

3. **Flexible compensation and benefits.** Does your organization:

   - ❑ Enable employees to achieve better work/life balance by making compensation and benefits clear, accessible, manageable, and valuable?
   - ❑ Make compensation part of a larger performance management system that motivates each employee to work toward high performance and business results?

Perspectives on Flexibility and Work/Life Balance

The challenge of balancing the needs of employee and employer has been addressed from many perspectives in the past. However, the emergence of a fiercely competitive, rapidly changing global economy and the growth of a Millennial workforce have increased the focus on this subject.

William Bridge's book, *JobShift: How to Prosper in a Workplace without Jobs,* raised some provocative and significant issues. The following points reflect the changing perspective on flexibility and work/life balance:

- **Traditional jobs are disappearing.**

  The traditional concept of a "job," with an eight-hour day, is quickly disappearing. A new organizational structure is emerging, based on projects that can often be completed without a traditional workday schedule and that might not even require "going to work."

- **We will all have to learn new ways to work.**

  Although the new ways of working will sometimes require new technological skills, they will more often require something more fundamental: the skill of finding and doing work in a world without clear-cut and stable jobs. Today's worker needs to look for work that needs doing.

- **Millennial workers are starting their careers with work/life plans in place.**

  People who are working on more than one project are already dividing their jobs into several pieces. The old policy of jobs—and job sharing—will be put into the Policy Museum as an artifact of a bygone age, and people will get on with doing the work that needs doing.

Alternative Work Schedules Are Now Required

In her book *Work Concepts for the Future: Managing Alternative Work Arrangements*, Patricia Schiff Estess addresses a basic yet underutilized concept: Has your organization moved from a more flexible scheduling strategy—often hush-hush in implementation—to chiseling formal, written policies on alternative work schedules into the corporate mission? As Estess states, "Even without a detailed cost-benefit analysis, alternative work arrangements that provide greater flexibility in the workplace and the hours people work have gone on for decades. Organizations know it is smart business to keep good employees by accommodating schedules as much as possible."

ALTERNATIVE WORK SCHEDULES: MILLENNIAL MOTIVATORS

Indicate which of the following statements (if any) are true.

Our organization has formally embraced the following flexible and alternative work schedules or policies:

____ 1. We embrace flextime as a win-win strategy for employer and Millennial.

____ 2. We achieve greater performance and productivity by condensing work into a compressed work week.

____ 3. Telecommuting is endorsed and encouraged.

____ 4. Job sharing has emerged as a viable and productive staffing structure.

____ 5. Reducing the work week has been introduced as a way of more effectively balancing work and personal life.

Millennials Are Starting Their Careers with Work/Life Plans in Place

The challenge of motivating the Millennial knowledge worker is not limited to private-sector corporations. Rather, this challenge has just as much of an impact on the public sector. As an example, the National Academy of Public Administration addressed this challenge in its 1998 publication titled *New Options, New Talent: The Government Guide to the Flexible Workforce*. It states that "Today's young workers are starting their careers with work/life balance in place. As a result … they want to spend more time with their families and realize the importance of having a life outside of work."

Recommendations for Action by Agencies and Their Managers

The authors of *New Options, New Talent*, while focusing on government organizations, provide recommendations for motivating the Millennial knowledge worker in both the public and private sectors, as follows.

1. **Think of the workforce as a multifaceted whole.**

   This approach requires that results-oriented strategic plans focus on all of the work to be accomplished, rather than on the number of workers.

2. **Use results rather than resources to measure performance.**

   The private and public sectors are moving toward a focus on results, rather than on the number of employees or equivalent managers. Refocus attention from headcounts to results.

3. **Identify a single official responsible for workforce policies and procedures.**

   Respond to the needs of the New Economy, which is characterized by more competitive, information-technology-driven services. This strategy requires a broader organizational and leadership commitment, coordination of organization policies, and cooperation of HR professionals and senior management.

Flexible Work Arrangements and Large-Scale Business Benefits

Addressing the motivational needs of Millennial knowledge workers through increased emphasis on flexibility and work/life balance is not a single workforce issue. Rather, it needs to be put into a broader perspective. As the authors of *Workforce Crisis* write, "There is a big difference between offering flexible arrangements to some workers and implementing flex work on a large scale that reaps business benefits."

Workforce Crisis Drives the Need for Flexible Work Arrangements

In his book *Generation Blend: Managing Across the Technology Age Gap*, Rob Salkowitz documents the convergence of three intriguing factors related to our evolving workforce and evolving work:

- A generational shift is underway across most of the developing world, as the cohort born after the end of World War II approaches retirement and a new generation of Millennials prepares to make its mark on the world.
- Experts predict that the demographic shift will make it more difficult for employers to find skilled workers to fill critical jobs.
- The ubiquity of technology raises the bar even higher. It means that workers will need to have deep knowledge of software, computers, and communication devices, even in jobs and industries that traditionally did not require those skills.

Salkowitz aptly describes the challenges that generational differences can and will make in a new world of work. And managing the different outlook of the tech-savvy Millennial college graduate can be a challenge. The freewheeling Millennial personal networking and communication style might have to be reconciled with more structured workplace requirements.

A Closer Look at Millennials and Their Need for Flexibility and Work/Life Balance

Today's Millennials are starting work with work/life balance in place and a pronounced need for flexibility. They have clearly developed motivational drivers that are critically important to them. These behavioral preferences will continue to challenge employee retention, recruiting, and management.

The following evaluation items are culled from Cam Marston's book, *Motivating the "What's In It for Me?" Workforce*, which reveals a broad spectrum of Millennial behavioral preferences that reinforce the importance of addressing flexibility and work/life balance and the need for proactive strategies.

A FLEXIBILITY AND WORK/LIFE BALANCE CHECKLIST

Identify which of the following behaviors characterize your Millennial knowledge workers' needs for flexibility and work/life balance.

____ 1. Millennials often measure an effective work ethic by whether they get the job done on time, not by how many hours they work each week.

____ 2. Technology is a freedom tool. It enables workers to complete their jobs faster and more easily, so they can get back to what's important—their lives outside the office.

____ 3. Gen X-ers say, "Get a life." New Millennials say, "I have a life. Work comes second."

____ 4. Millennial professionals like balance. These young adults value the good life, like their parents do, but are not willing to sacrifice time with family and friends to achieve it.

____ 5. Millennials are likely to want to build parallel careers, not focusing on one job or profession at the exclusion of others.

____ 6. Data consistently show that balance and flexibility are critical priorities for Millennials entering the workforce.

____ 7. Flexibility in planning a career around major life events is the most important element for achieving a good balance between a career and one's personal life.

____ 8. Work/life integration adds another dimension—not just the ability to do work from a life setting (e.g., at home or while doing life- and family-oriented activities), but the ability to participate in life from a work setting.

____ 9. Gen Y-ers are independent, techno-savvy, entrepreneurial hard workers who thrive on flexibility, and take these qualities to new heights or transform them.

Proactive Strategies Supporting Flexibility and Work/Life Balance

Flexibility and work/life balance are clearly interdependent Millennial motivators. However, in an effort to heighten the application potential for you, our reader/practitioner, the following discussion treats them separately. A combination of research-based recommendations and examples from our Contributing Experts further highlights selected concepts.

Flexibility: The Single Most Important Millennial Motivator

Contributing Expert Christopher R. Ryan, Deputy General Counsel, K12 Inc., captures the importance of this motivator in the following statement:

> ***"Millennial workers came of age in a world free from the previous time and space limitations on learning and working. Millennials seek flexibility in various dimension of their work life: in work hours (enable them to pursue outside interests), in work locations (e.g., telecommuting), and in the overall way that work fits into their lives. The concept that one can only be productive in the office between the hours of 9:00 AM and 6:00 PM is alien to Millennials. Facebook has replaced 'face time.' In order to attract and motivate Millennials, employers and managers must change their options on work and productivity and they must provide the necessary technology to enable this balance and flexibility."***

A Continuum of Flexibility Strategies

More specifically, there clearly appears to be a continuum of flexibility opportunities that line managers and human resources professionals can implement. These opportunities are presented in the following inventory, which you can use to identify your organization's current strengths and areas requiring further development.

1. **Flexibility in attendance and punctuality**

   Eric Chester, in *Employing Generation Why? Understanding, Managing, and Motivating Your New Workforce*, suggests that this generation isn't known for being punctual. And rather than lamenting about individuals arriving late and leaving early, you might do better to look both at corporate policies and at your personal work philosophy. In simplest terms, as our Contributing Experts also recommend, figure out what you really need from your employees. Often there are more opportunities for flexibility to be inserted into the workplace schedule.

2. **Implementing flexible work**

   Flexible scheduling is just a single component, or a tactic, of a much broader flexible work program. The authors of *Workforce Crisis* suggest the broader strategy of implementing a flexible work program in your organization. More specifically, they identify four key variables and suggest looking for situations in which all four variables are favorable. The four key variables are:

   - ▷ **The nature of the work** — How elastic is the work itself? Must it be performed at specific times or in specific places?
   - ▷ **Flexible-time programs** — Evaluate which positions are right for flexible hours and shifts. Define core business hours and the earliest start times and finish times.
   - ▷ **Reduced-time programs** — Evaluate which positions are right for reduced hours. Can you redistribute or reschedule work across existing resources, ensuring that workloads mesh with work times?
   - ▷ **Flexible-plan programs** — Evaluate which positions are right for mobile work or telecommuting. Can you install collaboration tools and ensure communication and connectedness for those people working off-site?

3. **Technology as a resource for Millennial flexibility and work/life balance**

   The growth of Millennial literature, research, and training programs parallels the rapid growth of this important workforce generation. Rob Salkowitz's recent book, *Generation Blend: Managing Across the Technology Age Gap,* presents a compelling case for technology further supporting the Millennials' priorities of flexibility and work/life balance. He states, "Millennials seek remote access and mobility, access to personal networks at work; standard accessible technology; two-way channels of internal communication; blogs and other channels of personal expression."

   The Millennials' use of technology to address both work and personal priorities on and off the job, while at times frustrating to managers, is emerging as a mutually beneficial resource.

Flexibility and Work/Life Balance: Examples

The motivational strategies and tactics presented in each part of this book are not mere academic recommendations. Rather, they are reflections of best-of-class practices. The following examples highlight the value of moving from concept to actual practice. They include a list of best practices, worker testimonials, and a final inventory of best practices.

The first snapshot of flexibility and work/life balance strategies and employee testimonials is just one example of the value of proactively addressing this motivational factor. The second short example highlights the importance of addressing the needs of working parents and other employees.

Creating an Environment Where People Come First

Shaara Roman, Director, Human Resources
CGI Federal

At CGI, we work together to create an environment where our people come first. We call our employees "members" to reinforce that all who join our team are, as owners, empowered to participate in the challenges and rewards that come from building a world-class company. We are one of the largest independent IT and business process services firms in the world, and our members are the key element of our continued success.

- **Telecommuting and flexible work schedules**

  To help employees save on travel costs and balance work and family, we offer our employees the opportunity to telecommute, as well as flexible work schedules. Both benefits are consistently praised by employees in our annual satisfaction survey. Part-time work arrangements and job sharing are also supported.

- **Member testimonials**

  We receive an overwhelming number of comments on CGI's commitment to work/life balance in our member satisfaction survey. For example:

  "I appreciate the flex time and how supportive managers are of staff utilizing flex time and vacation time to maintain work/life balance."

  "The freedom to work from where I need to when I need to is very important to me. The fact that I am able to remotely log into all my files and applications is important when I am traveling, as well as when I just have an idea at 8 p.m. at home and want to record it or send an email."

"When life happens, I've always been able to adjust my work hours to accommodate it."

"The ability to partially telecommute significantly increases my ability to help look after family members who have special needs."

Working Moms and Other Employees

Hector Velez, Executive Vice President
HireStrategy

First of all, we offer up to twelve weeks of maternity leave. Then, we encourage working mothers to telecommute at least one day a week. We have found that this has done wonders for morale and retention. Doing this cuts down on commuting time and allows the employee valuable time with her family. Another key to the success of this program has been the unconditional top-down support from the executive team. This support helps to alleviate the "guilt" factor that tends to seep into the employee's consciousness. From flextime and telecommuting to parental leave, we also try to expand the concept of family-friendly benefits to make sure they cover adoptive parents, fathers, and grandparents, as well as working mothers.

In addition, all HireStrategy employees are entitled to 120 hours (15 days) of leave each calendar year, which will accrue, pro-rated starting from the date of hire. Employees are encouraged to use their vacation each year; however, if they're unable to do so, up to one week can be carried over to the following year.

Finally, to enhance flexibility and productivity, we have created Web-enabled CRM technology so work can be done from any location with Internet access. We encourage employees to use the technology so that during off hours and when they're away from the office, they are "connected" and can maximize their performance.

Inventory of Flexible Workplace Policies

Kitty Nix, Director, Strategic Management
Helios HR

There are number of factors that are critical to building a culture focused on results while still encouraging flexibility and success for each employee. These factors include: a leadership team that models the way; business processes that focus on institutionalizing efficient product development and delivery models; and policies that reinforce the desire to provide flexibility while ensuring results. Following is a sample of some of these best-practice policies.

- **Management by Objectives (MBOs) performance metrics**

  Does your organization set individual objectives for all employees? Ideally, these objectives should stem from the organization's strategic plan. For example, for organizations providing professional services, does every employee have individualized utilization targets? These objectives should serve as the basis to hold employees accountable for results.

- **Core business hours**

  Does your business have core business hours? For example, do you mandate that all employees be accessible in person, via e-mail, or via cell phone between the hours of 9:30 to 4:30, but allow flexibility for some to work 7:30 to 5:00 while others work 9:30 to 6:00?

- **Paid time off**

  Do you group leave benefits into one bucket to maximize flexibility for employees? For example, do you have one policy that includes holidays, vacation time, and sick leave? This policy and the core-business-hours policies not only accommodate individual priorities, such as the need to celebrate different holidays, but also actually benefit the business by increasing customer access to your workforce.

- **Cell phone and data service reimbursement**

  Do you provide reimbursements for cell phones and data services so employees can be accessible while not in the office, such as for client meetings or for attending to personal business during the day?

- **Laptops**

  Do you provide laptops for all of your employees? You will find that employees are much more likely to go above and beyond the call of duty if they are equipped with tools that foster flexibility and allow them to work wherever they want.

- **Telecommuting, compressed work week, and job sharing**

  Do you encourage unique and individualized work arrangements that allow employees to address their non-work priorities? Many employees are interested in serving their community or actively participating in family responsibilities. Creating an environment that allows employees to reduce work hours, work remotely, or work fewer days can create employee loyalty that money cannot buy.

Not only do these policies foster a flexible environment, which helps to attract and retain the 21–30-year-old knowledge worker, but they also offer the opportunity to increase customer service. After all, happy employees are best equipped to serve customers.

Strategies for Work/Life Balance

The Millennial motivational factor of work/life balance is clearly a companion to the motivational factor of flexibility. It is one of the most significant priorities of the Millennial worker. There is, in fact, a clear generational progression in the importance of this motivational factor from Traditionalists to Boomers to Generation X to Millennials.

In the past, Traditionalists viewed work as the center of their life. The Boomers, while still influenced by the Traditionalist workaholic legacy, sought more balance in their lives. Generation X progressed further, as Rob Salkowitz states in *Generation Blend*, in "working to live, prioritizing lifestyle over career choices." And, finally, Millennials, accustomed to multitasking, simply view work as just one more thing to fit into their schedules.

The following model of previous generations' work/life relationships illustrates how work was viewed as the center of a worker's life in the past. Everything else (family, friends, entertainment, chores, vacation, community service, hobbies) merely revolved around the periphery.

Previous generations' work/life balance[1]

Work is Viewed Differently By Today's Workers

New Options, New Talent: The Government Guide to the Flexible Workplace, by the National Academy of Public Administration, discusses Gen X workers in the federal sector and describes a set of worker behaviors that clearly set the stage for Millennials moving work/life balance into their top-ten list of motivational factors. As an example, consider how many of the following Gen X preferences are now priorities for your Millennial workforce.

[1] Source: *New Options, New Talent: The Government Guide to the Flexible Workplace*, by the National Academy of Public Administration

- Today's workers no longer find security in a "lifetime" employer.
- "Work" and "lifetime employment" are no longer one and the same.
- Individuals have a different perspective on a one-employer career.
- Instead of finding security in an employer, people find security within themselves.
- Today's workers want to continue to learn in order to expand their skills, improving their marketability.
- For Generation X and Millennial workers, expanding their skills is comparable to purchasing disability insurance as a protection against accident or illness.

The employer- or work-centric model has been transformed, first by Boomers, then Gen Xers, and finally, Millennials into a balancing of work and life. As the following model illustrates, Work and Life now appear on a scale with emphasis on balance.

Younger generations' work/life balance[1]

The concept of "The Balance Scale" has been embraced and modified by organizational effectiveness and human resources professionals. Cam Marston, in *Motivating the "What's In It For Me? Workforce,"* suggests an interesting application of the concept. He presents a scale with two components: "Employee" on one side and "Company" on the other. He suggests using it as a motivational and communication tool between employee and manager. A short summary of his suggested application of this tool follows.

---

[1] Source: *New Options, New Talent: The Government Guide to the Flexible Workplace*, by the National Academy of Public Administration

The Employee and Company Scale: A Proactive Millennial Resource

In his book *Motivating The "What's In It For Me?" Workforce*, Cam Marston makes an important recommendation for managers of new Millennial employees. "As a manager, the thing to do is negotiate with your employees." More specifically, he introduces the concept of using the following Balance Scale to reconcile and balance Millennials' work/life needs with those of the organization.

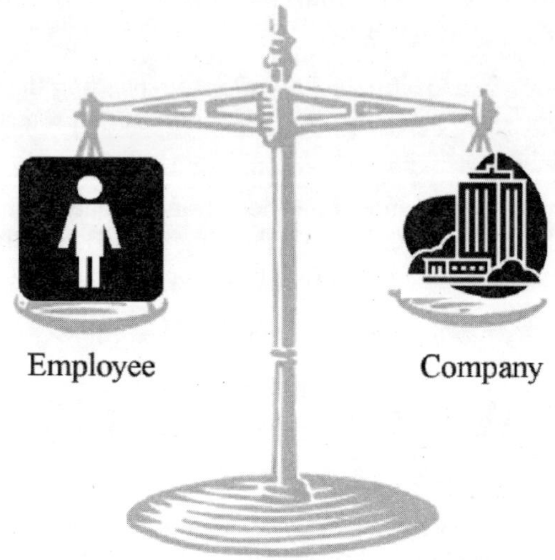

To effectively use the Employee and Company Scale, he makes the following recommendations.

- Give some thought to drawing this scale on paper when you talk with employees.
- Use it as a visual guide to show them how their needs must be balanced by the company's needs.
- Let employees see that the scale must remain level in order to serve customers, keep the company running, and allow everyone to be happy.
- Explain that employees become valuable when they are willing to work with their employer to keep the scale in balance.

The use of the scale will provide an opportunity to reconcile company needs with those work/life balance needs of the Millennial. This scale will also provide an opportunity for each individual to identify his or her own motivational and performance needs. It also provides an excellent opportunity to communicate with, negotiate with, and motivate the Millennial.

Further Discussion

Shira Harrington, Director, Professional Search Positions, Inc.

If we were to peer into the near future, we might be surprised to see the fulfillment of William Bridges' predictions that "Traditional jobs are disappearing." With the prevalence of remote technology, teleworking models, and the increased use of virtual communication, that day might come sooner than we think. There are two primary challenges, however, that must be overcome for this futuristic concept to become a reality: 1) a revamping of government and corporate regulations; and 2) a changing of old mindsets.

Revamping of Government and Corporation Regulations

Our current labor force is guided by restrictive, albeit often necessary, government regulations, such as the Fair Labor Standards Act, which mandates such distinctions as exempt vs. non-exempt employees. To retain the Millennial knowledge worker who, for example, may be classified as non-exempt but wants the flexibility to work creative (or even longer) hours, this can hinder a manager's ability to customize alternative working arrangements. Although created to protect workers during the industrial age, when hourly abuses were the norm, today these types of restrictive measures can impede employers from fostering an employee-centric talent management model. Advocacy organizations such as the Society for Human Resource Management should be encouraged to lobby for the repealing or revising of such laws in an effort to increase the opportunities for retaining a changing workforce.

Changing of Old Mindsets

Yet even with more flexible government and corporate policies in place, old mindsets must be changed as well. What originally generated a fascination in generational and age diversity was the struggle of older professionals to appreciate today's young workers' attitudes toward work-life integration, which are quite different from those of people who entered the workforce in the 1960s, '70s, and '80s. Further study should be conducted into ways that Veterans and Boomers can be sensitized not only to accept but also to champion flexible work arrangements without harboring a sour-grapes mentality because they were not afforded those opportunities when they were in their 20s. Although diversity training has been a good first step in creating awareness of the need for such accommodations, we are now ready for these older generations to embrace a complete shift of the mind, and of the heart, to engage an ambitious and demanding young workforce who must be retained in order for the company to remain competitive.

Summary

Millennials are keenly aware of the importance of flexibility and work/life balance. As Lisa Orrell writes in *Millennials Incorporated*, "They expect their manager and company to support and respect their lives outside of work." However, as managers address this pronounced need for work/life balance, they must also reconcile the organization's need to remain profitable in an increasingly competitive global economy. In addition, the Millennials' additional requirement for multidimensional growth opportunities, as discussed in the Part 2 of this book, further increases the challenge of meeting their motivational needs.

PART 2

Multidimensional Millennial Growth Opportunities

> *They [the Millennials] are looking for opportunities that empower them to use… time, tools, and their remarkable talents to build a better life… to have a job that means more than a paycheck and a life that really matters."*
>
> **–Eric Chester, *Employing Generation Why?***

In this part:

- Getting Started
- Multidimensional Growth Opportunities as Non-Negotiable Requirements
- Reconciling Growth Opportunities of Millennials with Knowledge Organizations
- Millennial Leadership Opportunities and Multidimensional Career Growth

Getting Started

A wide variety of responses resulted from a Contributing Expert–assisted preliminary survey of Millennial motivational factors. These included "career advancement, "challenging work," "fast cycle work environment," "quick promotions, and "personal goals." In addition, "learning, "training" and "technology" emerged high on the list of frequent responses. After an analysis of this data, some results were combined when definitions of similar factors emerged. The final Survey Analysis resulted in our creating eight parts of this book to discuss sixteen prominent motivational factors. Part Two, Multidimensional Growth Opportunities, is the result of this process. Emphasis is placed on the following four objectives:

- Appreciate that multidimensional growth opportunities are non-negotiable Millennial requirements
- Provide opportunities to reconcile Millennials' growth opportunities and the intellectual-capital needs of knowledge organizations
- Examine and apply Contributing Experts' strategies for implementing multidimensional growth opportunities
- Identify potential Millennial leaders through multidimensional growth opportunities

Multidimensional Growth Opportunities as Non-Negotiable Requirements

A theory of adult development pioneered by psychoanalyst Erik H. Erikson describes three stages of adulthood: intimacy (ages 21–35), generativity (ages 35–55), and integrity (age 55+). As Harry Levinson writes in "A Second Career: The Possible Dream" (in *Harvard Business Review On Work and Lift Balance*), Daniel Levinson's studies of executives "indicate that at about age 37, the adult throws off the guidance or protection of older mentors or managers and takes full charge of himself." Daniel Levinson calls this "the BOOM [becoming one's own man] effect," and it can drive people to seek new careers.

By curious counterpoint, our Millennials "want it all now." As Martin and Tulgan write in *Managing Generation Y*:

> ***"Organizations that can't—or won't—customize training, career paths, incentives, and work responsibilities need a wake-up call."***

They further state:

> ***"This generation won't be lured by promises of climbing ladders, paying dues, and cashing out at retirement. They want to know:***
>
> ***— What value can I add today?***
>
> ***— What can I learn today?***
>
> ***— What will you offer me today?***
>
> ***— How will I be rewarded today?"***

A quick review of current Millennial literature indicates a recurring priority: Millennials have a strong need for ongoing multidimensional growth opportunities.

How Does Your Organization Meet Millennials' Growth Needs?

Identify which of the following motivational needs your organization addresses effectively, and which ones require more attention.

____ 1. "The Millennial Professional tends to be very demanding (of themselves and others) and understands that it is their responsibility to work hard to get what they want… This ambition and desire for 'success and rewards' has been in them from birth, with Boomer or Gen-X parents telling them they can do anything they put their minds to." (*Millennials Incorporated*)

____ 2. "For them [Millennials], life is an all-you-can-eat buffet offering unlimited choice, few rules, and a pay-as-you-go system… [T]hey believe in their ability to leapfrog over the painstaking cultivate/plant/fertilize parts and go directly to the harvest." (*Employing Generation Why?*)

____ 3. "Because Gen Yers grew up with interactive media that combined education with fun, they expect learning to be part of their daily lives. They want to experience clear connections between the skills they learn today and the skills they will use tomorrow." (*Managing Generation Y*)

____ 4. "Leaders with a knowledge perspective can see alternative career patterns for professionals, patterns that often involve new experiences, travel, and changes of work—including changing career tracks. Successful knowledge organizations know their professionals so well that they can plan this kind of career for them." (*The New Organizational Wealth: Managing and Measuring Knowledge-based Assets*)

If there is one assumption that line managers and human resources professionals must unequivocally embrace, it is that multidimensional opportunities are non-negotiable Millennial requirements.

Reconciling Millennial Growth Opportunities with Knowledge Organizations

A variety of strategic initiatives appear to be coming together that not only leverage the talent of a multigenerational workforce, but also propel the "new Millennials" as an emerging component of a responsive "New Economy." As the authors of *Workforce Crisis: How to Beat the Coming Shortage of Skills and Talents* recommend:

> ***"What many young people need most to feel happy in a company is the continuous opportunity to learn and grow through frequent changes in roles, responsibilities, and programs."***

The authors go on to state:

> ***"Challenge them, stretch them, stimulate them, let them try new things, allow them to learn by doing and failing—if you can do these things, you will keep more of the young talent you have."***

Interestingly, there is increasingly more evidence that the growth opportunities for both Millennial knowledge workers and their respective organizations can employ complementary strategies. Several conceptual building blocks are discussed next, followed by examples of multidimensional growth opportunities provided by our Contributing Experts.

FORCES SHAPING THE AMERICAN ECONOMY

The Hudson Institute's publication *Workforce 2020: Work and Workers in the 21st Century* identifies five forces that will change the face of the American economy. Indicate which of the forces are most relevant to your organization, with 1 being the most relevant and 5 being the least relevant.

____ 1. Rapid technological change

____ 2. Further global integration of the U.S. economy

____ 3. Rapid economic growth in certain developing nations

____ 4. Deregulation and liberalization, both nationally and globally

____ 5. Demographic change, especially in the aging of the Baby Boomers

Clearly, rapid technological change, especially during the aging of the Baby Boomers, will create both winners and losers among industries, companies, and occupations. The growing number of Millennial knowledge workers will be willing to job-hop for better positions to remain on the winning side of the employment equation.

The New Economy as a Knowledge Economy

Frances Horibe, writing in *Managing Knowledge Workers: New Skills to Unlock the Intellectual Capital in Your Organization*, describes the New Economy as a "…flood of information coming at lightning speed" that is "changing almost everything. How we buy, how we sell, what we make, when we make it, what we value, and where we live." As she concludes the preface to her book, she makes five key points that are directly relevant to the Millennial knowledge worker:

- "The driver of success in the New Economy is knowledge."
- "Demand for knowledge workers is great and growing."
- "A knowledge worker is one who uses her head more than her hands to produce value."
- "About 60 per cent of all jobs are knowledge-based."
- "Managing the human dimension of knowledge work is the most important job a manager has."

The Millennials and Organizational Learning

Becoming a learning organization benefits all employees regardless of their generation, occupations, and education. However, as many of our reader/practitioners appreciate, organizations must expand the scope of learning. In the 1990s, organizations emphasized getting out of the "business of training" and into the "business of learning and performance." Now, as the authors of *Workforce Crisis* remind us, "Learning isn't a specialist activity in HR—it's a core management issue, a leadership responsibility, and an employee responsibility."

In a learning organization, learning takes place on a 24/7 basis, up, down, and across the organizational ladder, in classrooms, in hallways, online, and over a cup of coffee. Dychtwald, Erickson, and Morison suggest that organizational learning can be thought of as a three-legged stool. This concept is most relevant to the learning needs of Millennial knowledge workers.

ORGANIZATIONAL LEARNING

Indicate which of the following motivational needs your organization addresses effectively, and which require more attention.

My organization:

____ 1. Realizes individual career and growth plans, orchestrating work assignments (especially stretch assignments) and training experiences to accomplish them.

____ 2. Ensures the right mix of skills and the right behaviors for learning company wide.

____ 3. Establishes connections among people who can productively teach, learn from each other, and share information with one another.

____ 4. Progresses from passive directories of expertise and experience to active "communities of practice."

____ 5. Improves individual and network knowledge and capability.

____ 6. Delivers useful content and experience to develop specific capabilities.

____ 7. Provides courses conducted in person or virtually, plus on-the-job instruction and certification.

Multidimensional Growth Opportunities at CGI Federal

Shaara Roman, HR Director
CGI Federal

At CGI, we strive to create an environment that promotes the professional development of our members and facilitates and encourages the exchange of expertise among them. This enables us to continue to meet the quality needs of the marketplace. CGI understands the need to maintain and enhance our members' technical and managerial knowledge and skills on an ongoing basis. Our training and professional development programs ensure that this need is met.

Members of CGI are responsible for setting their career objectives and pursuing their professional development in a manner consistent with the company's goals and objectives. We recognize that an employee's growth and development comprise a combination of ongoing project opportunities, formal training programs, and coaching and mentoring.

Ongoing Project Opportunities

CGI is in the business of delivering projects, which afford our members unlimited opportunities to develop skills and pursue career advancement. Most members are part of project teams that are structured to provide support and training from teammates at all levels. In addition, our employees have the opportunity to work on numerous projects throughout their careers, with each project providing its own opportunities for learning. A significant percentage of our members begin at the ground level of project work and advance up the management ladder as they gain skills and experience.

Formal Training Programs

We offer a variety of professional, technical, and leadership training to employees within our company.

- **CGI 101**

  An intensive four-day leadership training seminar that covers CGI from A to Z, including the company's philosophy, values, business methodologies, and frameworks. Attendees have an opportunity to meet CGI's senior executives, listen to presentations from leaders of key operational areas, learn CGI's management processes, and network. This program is currently available to managers and above when they join CGI or are promoted, but will soon be made available to all CGI members.

- **Project Leaders Development Track**

  This comprehensive training course educates members on all aspects of successful project delivery with the goal of increasing CGI's success rate in delivering projects on time, on budget, and in line with client expectations.

- **Guided Tour**

  This e-learning tool provides members with a virtual tour of CGI as a whole, including our operations, practices, and culture. It also points members to a variety of resources on our enterprise portal. The tool also features a feedback mechanism, allowing members to ask questions and offer suggestions.

- **Personal Development Kiosk**

  More than 29,000 hours of classroom instruction were delivered to CGI members in 2008. Each employee has a key to a Personal Development Kiosk, which provides 24/7 access to an extensive library of business and technical courses and publications. Employees can integrate training and information access into their workout routines or commutes by downloading courses to an MP3 player for training on the go.

- **Next-Level Leadership Program**

  We understand that a large part of a member's satisfaction and engagement rests in the hands of his or her leaders. To promote better leadership, we offer a learning cohort training program to help up-and-coming executives "step up" to the next level by learning how to empower their teams, communicate a vision, and broaden their footprint in the organization. We have seen how this program benefits not only our future leaders, but also the teams they work with.

- **Tuition Reimbursement**

  We provide tuition reimbursement to members with outstanding performance who are building their careers at CGI. This reimbursement can range from a select course to the pursuit of a degree.

Mentoring/Coaching

The third element of a member's growth and development comes from informal and formal mentoring/coaching programs. All new employees are assigned a mentor for their first year to enhance the integration and assimilation process. We have also recognized the value of a formal mentoring/coaching program to help our employees navigate their careers and get guidance and informal learning from someone other than their manager. In the CGI Federal Business Unit, we are preparing to launch a formal mentoring program to provide mentoring relationships that will focus on specific development needs identified by the employee.

Multidimensional Growth Opportunities at The Urban Institute

Deborah K. Hoover, HR Director
The Urban Institute

At The Urban Institute, we have worked hard over a number of years to provide a culture of support that recognizes young professionals' needs and desires for growth, accomplishment, and responsibility. This is most particularly true for policy researchers, the core of our workforce. Whether straight out of academic programs or after a few years of experience, our recruits have several things in common—they are highly accomplished, they possess high levels of intrinsic motivation, and they want to make a difference at work and beyond very quickly. In many ways, they are the very model of the Millennial knowledge worker.

Due to the researchers' centrality to our mission, our human resources policies and programs, our managerial practices, and the organizational culture as a whole have developed in such a way as to feed the very needs for which Millennials are known. Outward signs of our support for their needs can be found throughout the organization. The following table provides numerous examples of our approach to job, career, professional, and personal growth. Throughout, we underscore the continuing need for learning and application of knowledge, support and rewards for growth and accomplishment, and the idea that responsibility includes leadership. By maintaining high expectations and establishing clear indicators of accomplishment, we give Millennial staffers a clear sense of the "Urban" experience—what they must give and what, in turn, they will take away from this experience.

A Multidimensional, Integrated Approach to Growth

	Programs and policies include:	Effective supervisors and managers provide:	How an organization's culture reflects attitudes on growth
Job growth	Best-in-class tuition assistance program Financial support for conference attendance, outside seminars, and professional association memberships In-house learning communities Brown-bag seminars	Mentoring Opportunities to work in small teams Exposure to multiple projects	Adjectives used to describe the environment: collegial, collaborative, decentralized "My job is as big as I want it to be." Multidisciplinary teams
Career growth	Written standards for performance, promotion, and salary determinations Open job search process A formal salary and promotion process Staff-wide announcements of promotions	Opportunities to collaborate meaningfully with senior scholars Authority and responsibility for project deliverables Expectation of greater independence over time Exposure to external stakeholders	Recognized research career ladder that is consistent with sister research institutions Pragmatic policy interpretation that recognizes unique circumstances and individuals Managerial willingness to coach and explain
Professional growth	Formal committees responsible for reviewing individual accomplishments Access to leadership training opportunities Participation in organizational decision-making through employee committees Annual "Best-in Class Research Awards" Employee-led "RAA Discussion Series"	Facilitation of external relationships with funders, outside scholars, government representatives, and other stakeholders Opportunities to lead project teams Financial support and paid time for professional development activities	Statements from staff, e.g., "To get ahead in research, you really need an advanced degree." Physical office space supports small and large conferences, enabling researcher participation at all levels In-house research library services UI Summer Academy for Public Policy Analysis & Research
Personal growth and social interactions	In-house personal development seminars Employer-sponsored parties, networking, and recreational activities Employer-sponsored charitable activities supporting the larger community In-house workout facility Alumni network	Role-modeling through attendance and participation in all activities	From several exit interviews, "The thing I've liked the best about my time here is that I've grown up." Physical office space includes many small and less formal group spaces where staff chat, read, and eat lunch An open-door policy all the way to the executive suite Very few "employee class" distinctions Annual team building allowance for each work group

The Booz Allen Hamilton Career Planning Services Model

Stacey Kessel, Career Planning Senior Manager
Booz Allen Hamilton

Booz Allen Hamilton's career planning services serve more than 18,000 employees worldwide. Given the diversity of needs, we designed service offerings that could be self-directed and accessed via a website. We also offer enhanced and customized career planning and mentoring services for strategic employee groups such as staff with highly marketable skills.

Model Development

The model design was validated through benchmarking, internal surveys, interviews, and focus groups. A broad representation of leaders across the firm collaborated on the design. Client staff as well as people-services colleagues (HR, Recruiting, and Learning and Development) provided input that helped shape the services model.

Managers' self-assessments of skills, attitudes, and actual behavior on career development gave us their perspective on their responsibilities and ways to successfully support them. For example, managers said they did not want to attend training to build their career coaching skills, but rather would benefit from hearing about their peers' best practices. In focus groups with top-performing employees, we heard a consensus that successful employees take responsibility for driving their own careers.

The Career Planning Services Framework

Taking into consideration both manager and employee perspectives, we framed our Career Planning Services as a means to strengthen the partnership between employees and managers, and we offer services and support tailored to both groups. Additionally, to facilitate the sharing of best practices, we have leveraged technology (website, blogs, wikis, etc.) and developed online tools that allow managers to collaborate with each other regarding people development. In this online environment, managers can collaborate and share best practices. As noted, Career Planning Services reaches all of the firm's 18,000 employees. While the resources and tools are accessible to staff at all levels, they are particularly geared to administrative professionals up to director-level staff.

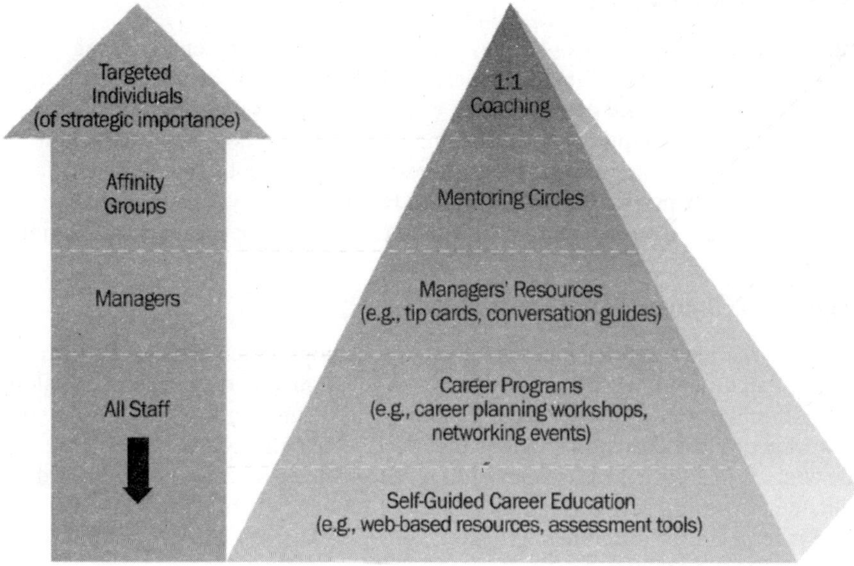

The Career Planning Services framework at Booz Allen Hamilton

Innovative Services

Our Career Planning Services are innovative in terms of balancing the business needs of our firm with the individual career interests, goals, and passions of our employees. Traditionally, candid career discussions of "Where do you see yourself in five years?" occur solely in the interview phase. Our firm-wide "Take 5" campaign encourages managers and employees to dedicate time for ongoing discussions on career development, and encourages the development of multiple mentoring relationships to support career planning goals. The objective is that as employees' interests and plans grow and develop, managers can adapt and integrate information about business direction to ensure that careers are aligned with the firm. The results are stronger connectivity between employees and managers, an improved sense of clarity regarding career options within the firm, and ultimately, improved engagement levels.

Beyond "Career Pathing"

In addition, our practice goes well beyond "career pathing" by encouraging employees to explore all of their interests, both those directly related to their day jobs and others that could be considered extracurricular. We have adopted a philosophy of "job sculpting" and coaching employees on how to "mold" their current positions to better reflect their interests. This concept, created by Dr. James Waldrop and Dr. Timothy Butler of Harvard Business School, is an innovative approach to career development in the context of the employee-employer setting.

Response to Changing Demographics

Lastly, our service offerings meet the changing demographic needs of the firm. Because a significant number of staff work on location at client sites, we developed a suite of online, self-directed career planning and mentoring tools and resources (vs. workshops and coaching sessions that need to be delivered in person). We offer three courses in a virtual-classroom setting accessible by staff across the world to facilitate networking across the firm's many offices and client sites. And each course is targeted for different segments of our population: Gen X/Y and/or those with significant work experience.

Multitude of Learning Solutions and Delivery Services

Our Career Services Model reflects a careful balance of employee and manager needs, the best interests of the firm, and best practices in the industry. Tailoring the services to our culture, the model incorporates a multitude of learning solutions and delivery methods. It provides:

- A framework of services driven by customer needs analysis
- A vehicle to educate employees on career opportunities within the firm
- A host of resources for managers to engage in effective career conversations with staff
- A program for enhancing the culture of mentoring throughout the firm

Millennial Leadership Opportunities and Multidimensional Career Growth

Providing multidimensional growth opportunities for Millennials benefits both individual and organization. In addition, evidence from an increasingly greater number of researchers indicates that multidimensional career growth opportunities for a new "hero" generation will benefit society at large.

Generational Personalities

William Strauss's and Neil Howe's now classic book *Generations: The History of America's Future* introduced the concept of generational personalities and went on to develop a methodology for assessing, explaining, and forecasting the ways that generational factors can and will influence future historical events. The authors take this concept a step further in suggesting that predictable cycles of social dynamics will repeat themselves.

Almost a decade later, Strauss and Howe published *Millennials Rising: The Next Great Generation*. Their enthusiasm for this group, often called the new "hero" generation, is apparent in the following statement:

> ***"As a group, Millennials are unlike any other youth generation in living memory. They are more numerous, more affluent, better educated, and more ethnically diverse… Over the next decade, the Millennial Generation will entirely recast the image of youth from downbeat and alienated to upbeat and engaged—with potential seismic consequences for America."***

Meeting the multidimensional career needs can benefit society and the New Economy on a variety of levels. Most important, "When Millennials hit the workforce in significant numbers, they are going to shake things up with their numbers, their collective purpose, and their global perspective; they can't help but transform the workplace and the world" (*Generation Blend*).

Investing in Millennial Leadership Potential

Investing in developing Millennial leadership potential has emerged as a clearly defined body of literature. A new book, *Millennial Leaders: Success Stories From Today's Most Brilliant Generation Y Leaders,* by Bea Fields, Scott Wilder, Jim Bunch, and Rob Newbold, present well-documented case histories of the proven leadership track record of the new "hero" generation.

Sue McLeod, a Hay Group, Inc., Contributing Expert, presents the following research-based summary, which points out the importance of multidimensional career growth opportunities for Millennials. More specifically, Hay Group, Inc., has identified four growth characteristics of people with high potential for leadership positions. This short summary captures still another important Millennial dimension.

Investing in Potential

Sue McLeod, Senior Consultant
Hay Group

We know that it pays off to develop your high-potential employees and do what you can to keep them. And we know that the younger generation wants continuous development and increasing challenge. But how can you tell which employees are high potentials, worthy of your investment? Our research identified four growth characteristics of people with potential for leadership positions:

- Social understanding and empathy
- Curiosity and eagerness to learn
- Emotional balance, resilience, and realistic optimism
- Thinking beyond the boundaries—a disposition to look beyond their role and make connections between their ideas and others.

There are also factors that are often used to assess leadership potential, but are, in fact, not such good indicators:

- Being the very best performer in the current job
- Expressing great personal ambition and drive

Further Discussion

Shira Harrington, Director, Professional Search Positions, Inc.

Several important issues remain that merit further consideration.

How do smaller organizations tackle the challenge of providing ongoing learning opportunities when financial and staff resources do not allow for corporate universities or even a human resources staff to design comprehensive learning and development programs?

What are the practical implications of these learning opportunities? Are employees given sufficient working hours to participate in these programs, or are they required to use personal learning time? Millennials will generally push back if asked to use their free time for work-related activities.

How receptive are supervisors to being trained on coaching and mentoring methods? In particular, Generation X managers tend to be adverse toward coaching and mentoring Millennial workers since they generally reject such performance management for themselves.

Will corporations utilize virtual learning models such as Second Life, which are currently being implemented by such progressive companies as IBM and Microsoft, in order to facilitate collaboration and learning between remote locations?

As Millennials age and change their marital and/or family status, how will this affect their ability to take advantage of training programs that may require them to learn during their personal time? Generation X knowledge workers are well aware of this challenge, as they are now of the age to have families themselves.

How are employers using their learning programs to develop succession planning models in light of the short tenure of Millennials, which averages 18 months according to the Bureau of Labor Statistics? What implications does this have for their future growth into executive leadership?

What types of courses are being designed to shore up basic competencies such as writing, oral communication, problem solving, and conflict resolution, since these are areas in which Millennials are generally weak?

Finally, how are organizations developing pairing models in their mentoring programs? Are they teaming retiring Veteran and older Boomer populations with Millennials, who tend to be hungry to learn from their "elders"? Are employers capitalizing on the institutional knowledge of these seasoned employers to stave off the inevitable brain drain?

Summary

Part Two objectives focused on appreciating that multidimensional growth opportunities are non-negotiable Millennial requirements; providing opportunities to reconcile these growth opportunities and the knowledge organization's intellectual capital needs; examining and applying Contributing Experts' strategies for providing multidimensional growth opportunities; and identifying potential Millennial leaders through these growth opportunities.

As we move on to Part Three, Fun and Social Interaction, we have an opportunity to further discuss a significant Millennial motivational factor. For the Millennial, there is a clear and concurrent blending of advancing one's career, learning new competencies and skills, and having fun in a highly social setting at the same time. This is a fascinating generation that has moved work/life balance from a desirable to an essential attribute of the new workplace.

PART 3

Fun and Social Interaction

> ***"Virtually every piece of research about Generation Why (Millennials) highlights the importance they place on fun. What may be surprising is the extreme importance Generation Why places on having fun on the job."***
>
> **–Eric Chester, *Employing Generation Why?***

In this part:

- Getting Started
- Fun and Social Interaction: Important Motivational Factors
- Managers and HR Professionals Need to Employ "Millennial Fun" Strategies
- Managers and HR Professionals Need to Increase Millennial Social Interaction
- Fun and Social Interaction: Examples

Getting Started

As with previous parts of this book, this part is driven by our survey of Millennial motivational factors. Responses that are relevant to this part include the value Millennials place on "managers' treatment of Millennials as colleagues," "interest in employees," "enjoyment," "humor," flexibility," and "growth." After analyzing the data, we combined similar factors. "Fun" received the fifth highest frequency of responses, and "social interaction" was close behind, as the seventh most important motivational factor. As a result, these two companion motivational factors were combined into this section.

This part focuses on the following four objectives:

- Recognize that fun and social interaction are significant motivational factors that must be acknowledged and valued as a human capital asset.
- Encourage managers and human resources professionals to incorporate strategies for the motivational factor of fun into the workplace.
- Identify organizational opportunities for incorporating technology-based and non-technology-based social interaction strategies into the workplace.
- Provide Contributing Experts' best-of-class strategies for expanding opportunities for fun and social interaction.

Fun and Social Interaction: Important Motivational Factors

As Rebecca Huntley writes in *The World According to Why: Inside the New Adult Generation,* "In order to understand why they are who they are, we need to understand their past, the world they were born into and grew up in." And while the focus of this book does not allow for a more historical generational analysis, we can look forward and describe select behaviors of what is clearly the largest youth generation in history, encompassing more than 80 million people in the United States.

They are described, in part, as adaptable, innovative, efficient, resilient, tolerant, and committed. Eric Chester, writing in *Employing Generation Why?,* states that "Ready or not, here comes Generation Why. And they're not politely knocking—they're breaking down the door. They are entering the workforce—and society—with a whole new set of attitudes, values, and beliefs."

Furthermore, Millennials expect their work environment to be fun and to provide them with a continuum of varied social interactions and even, as Martin and Tulgan write, "infinitely thrilling opportunities."

The Role and Responsibility of Managers and Human Resources Professionals

Gaining an appreciation of the importance of the motivational factors of fun and social interaction is a shared responsibility of manager, human resources professional, Millennial, and organization. There are obviously a variety of ways we can learn from each other.

From my perspective as educator and consultant, I find that Millennials are helping us rediscover what we once experienced in childhood. When you observe children at play, you become aware that in one sandbox or school-yard experience, they combine learning, play, creativity, and fun. Unfortunately, as many of us grew up—certainly the older generations—we came to understand that we "learned" in school, "played" in the park," and "had fun" in still another location.

In contrast, Gen Yers grew up with interactive media combining education and fun, so they are accustomed to learning as part of their daily lives. They are used to having unlimited options and few rules. They want high levels of fun and social interaction now, on the job, and 24/7.

In taking a closer look at the previously described set of Millennial expectations, we can see that there is actually a positive and productive correlation between Millennials' need for immediate fun and social interaction and an organization's performance expectations. A review of the following organizational inventory reinforces this observation.

FUN AND SOCIAL INTERACTION: AN ORGANIZATIONAL INVENTORY

Indicate which Millennial motivational factors your organization currently recognizes and supports, and which factors require more attention.

____ 1. "Generation Why doesn't just love fun; they are addicted to it… There is absolutely no doubt that Gen Why has no interest in a working environment that is not heavy on fun." (From *Employing Generation Why?*)

____ 2. "There's virtually no limit to what organizations will do to energize their teams with fun—and usually low-cost activities." (From *Managing the Generation Mix*)

____ 3. "If you can create an environment which is always pushing the envelope, gives people a fair amount of autonomy, involves them in decisions that affect them, and make it a fun place to work, you can create a center of excellence." (From *Managing Knowledge Workers)*

____ 4. "Human capital is the ultimate business asset. The organization with the better workforce wins. But don't equate better with skills and expertise. Human capital has three dimensions, all of which factor in the performance equation."

- Intellectual capital is what people know and learn.
- Social capital is how people form connections and share.
- Emotional capital is how much people are committed to the organization and how much of themselves they're willing to invest in its success. (From *Workforce Crisis*)

Fun and social interaction will be shown to be critically important Millennial motivational factors. In addition, they will be presented as readily accessible resources for line managers and human resources professionals. Remember, "The organization with the better workforce wins."

The Manager's Role as "Ringmaster of Fun" or "Millennial Empowerer"

While there is no doubt that Millennials place great emphasis on having fun in the workplace, "fun provider" might not be an easy leadership role for all managers to support. From a generational perspective, we know that Boomers (those individuals approximately 45–61 years old), according to Eric Chester, "believe that work is a sacrifice you make in order to enjoy life away from work. Boomers are willing to work long hours, to struggle to succeed, and to take pride in the status of difficult, involving, and high-paying jobs."

In addition, Rick Humphress, a Contributing Expert for this book, reminds us that we should also be cautious about generalizing about generational behavioral differences, when examining sociological differences is only one method of viewing behavior. He further states that when organizations apply broader talent management practices based on specific worker temperaments or types (e.g., the Myers-Briggs Type Indicator), the worker populations can be divided into sixteen categories. Taking the concept a step further, instead of thinking in terms of four generational classifications, we can suggest that there may be as many as sixteen behavioral types for each generational classification.

The point in presenting this concept is take the pressure off of managers so they don't have to think of themselves, as Eric Chester describes, as "having to be the guru of workplace fun." Instead of serving as the "guru" or "ringmaster," the manager can serve as an "empowerer of Millennials" to set the scene for incorporating fun in the workplace. The following inventory provides an opportunity for reader/practitioners to identify their own strengths and areas for development as empowerers of Millennials.

Managers Walk the "Fun" Talk: An Inventory

Indicate which of the following behaviors you personally model for your Millennial workers, and which behaviors require more attention.

____ 1. "[I know that] in the eyes of the Millennial Professional, [my] credibility and respect level will skyrocket if [I] not only manage them with friendliness, but [manage] with a sense of humor (and humanness), as well." (From *Millennials Incorporated*)

____ 2. "[I] help Gen-Yers find the fun in work, such as learning new skills, building relationships with impressive people, and achieving tangible results they can put their name on." (From *Managing Generation Y*)

____ 3. "[As an] effective manager I search for innovative ways to incorporate fun into their workplace, realizing that this serves them well on several fronts." (From *Employing Generation Why?*)

____ 4. "[I] find ways to recognize and reward desired behaviors and then celebrate them." (From *Motivating the "What's in it for Me?" Workforce*)

____ 5. "[I recognize that] centers of excellence are almost always fun places to be—not just exciting work environments—but actually fun. So how do you do it?" (From *Managing Knowledge Workers*)

____ 6. "[I understand that] Millennials just want to have fun—at work… They look to the workplace as a social organization, not just a job." (From *The Trophy Kids Grow Up*)

Managers and HR Professionals Need to Employ "Millennial Fun" Strategies

The following three strategies range from the most basic to the more comprehensive. Each strategy is followed by specific tactics that you can select and employ as relevant to your needs. A final Action Plan appears at the end of this section to further heighten application potential.

Strategy One: Establish a Climate for Fun and Social Interaction

The following recommendations, from *Managing Generation Y*, offer a good starting point for the manager wanting to enhance a climate of fun and social interaction.

- **Create a comfortable, low-stress environment.**

  There is absolutely no question, based on solid research, that Millennials find as the primary cause of stress, not the work itself, but the non-collegial management style of their supervisor. Proven "Millennial de-motivators" are managers who yell (hard to believe,) treat them as kids (unforgiveable,) and make unreasonable demands (poor management skills.) A comfortable, low-stress environment can be created by a manager providing feedback in a constructive way, making the Millennial feel comfortable, and in general presenting an easygoing and laid-back interpersonal style.

- **Focus on work, but be personable and have a sense of humor.**

  Contrary to misconceptions, Millennials do not want an all-fun, no-work environment. On the contrary, they respect a manager who can be serious and professional about work, but at the same time have a sense of humor, risk vulnerability, and maintain a creative and upbeat environment.

- **Spend time getting to know your team and their capabilities.**

  Managing knowledge and human capital is not a mere systems process, but rather is part of a broader human equation. While the following recommendations may appear to be drawn from a Basic Supervision 101 training course, they are nonetheless too often overlooked.

  - Capitalize on informal "getting-to-know-you timeouts." Get ready for spontaneous brainstorming or coaching sessions..
  - Encourage staff members to talk about what's important to them, what's on their minds.

- ▷ Plan one-on-one meetings on a consistent basis (weekly or at least biweekly).
- ▷ Encourage Gen Yers to create and maintain an achievement file or career portfolio. This is not only a great morale booster for them, but a useful tool for you.

In summary, providing opportunities to get to know your Millennial staff as colleagues, team members, and unique individuals is a sound basis for establishing a climate for fun and social interaction.

Strategy Two: Having Fun Can Start Small

For some readers/practitioners, it may be easier to recognize and appreciate the importance of the Millennial motivation factors of fun and social interaction than to implement an actual strategy. However, "having fun" in the workplace does not have to be an elaborate or complicated process. In *Managing Knowledge Workers*, Frances Horibe describes several rules of thumb that Barb MacCallum of Careerware put in place, which increased both employee retention and customer satisfaction. Here are her simple and effective suggestions:

- ▶ **Find a fun person to put in charge of events.**

  By identifying the right person to provide leadership for this initiative, you not only lighten your work load; you are also giving the task to someone who may be better suited to create fun and excitement.

- ▶ **Use the employees' standard of fun, not the manager's.**

  Even a fundamental understanding of generational attributes will quickly delineate differences in the core values, assets, and work styles of Boomers, Generation Xers, and Millennials. What may be fun for a Boomer may not be fun for a Millennial.

- ▶ **It doesn't have to be big or expensive, but it does have to include everyone.**

  Initiating a variety of corporate fun initiatives does not have to be a resource-intensive activity (time, budget, etc.). But as Contributing Expert examples will soon suggest, there needs to be a broad variety of fun and social interaction activities that are modest in cost. The activities should also be ones that everyone not only can participate in, but also want to participate in.

The previous three suggestions are presented as an accessible starter kit. It is intended as a low-risk, high-reward Millennial motivational strategy.

Strategy Three: Implementing a Multidimensional Fun Strategy

The Motivational Factors Survey that was used to shape the contents of this book clearly placed "fun" in the top-ten list of Millennial motivators. And the fact that almost any book on Millennials, knowledge workers, and managing the mix of generations addresses the subject of fun further reinforces the importance of this motivational factor.

Perhaps the most thorough and strategic treatment of the subject appears in Eric Chester's book *Employing Generation Why? Understanding, Managing, and Motivating Your New Workforce*. In his book, he states, "Generation Why doesn't just love fun; they're addicted to it… For them, work is no different from going to school or a friend's house or even an amusement park." Here are Chester's three suggestions:

1. **"Make fun through competition."**

   "Appeal to the game playing nature of Gen Y. They absolutely love to compete, especially when the winner is recognized and rewarded." However: "Be leery of contests where employees continually compete against each other for a single prize. Instead, get them to support each other by pitting them against a very achievable goal where everyone eventually does the victory dance."

2. **"Make fun through participation."**

   "When Generation Why is participating, they're engaged. When they're not, they're disengaged. It's that simple. Companies that learn how to appeal to their innate desire to express themselves through creative participation in the process … find that they can capture the soul and release the imagination of a very inventive resource." Eric Chester adds, "Find a way to point a spotlight in their direction, and you'll get a command performance."

3. **"Make fun through interaction."**

   "Today's … members of Gen Why are starting to demand social interaction. … As a result, Generation Why is trying to compensate by seeking jobs where they can work alongside their friends and where social interaction isn't penalized." "Instead of being the ringmaster, empower your young employees to create their own fun by simply providing an atmosphere conducive to social interaction."

Continuing Expert best-of-class examples and research suggest that when a sense of fun and social interaction is introduced into a workplace, and this is balanced with a clear delineation of roles and responsibilities, both Millennials and their organizations benefit.

A "FUN" ACTION PLAN

Review each of the following nine tactics and indicate which are the most relevant to your organization's efforts to employ fun and social interaction as motivators.

____ 1. Create a comfortable, low-stress environment.

____ 2. Focus on work, but be personable and have a sense of humor.

____ 3. Spend time getting to know your team members and their abilities.

____ 4. Find a "fun" person and put him or her in charge of events.

____ 5. Use the employees' standard of fun, not the manager's.

____ 6. It doesn't have to be big or expensive, but it does have to include everyone.

____ 7. Create fun through competition.

____ 8. Create fun through participation.

____ 9. Create fun through interaction.

There is an infinite number of ways to enhance the "Fun Factor." The most important concept is that you are embracing the concept as a strategy that not only enhances the quality of the workplace, but also unlocks the intellectual capital of your organization. This turns impending demographic challenges—a deficit of younger workers—into a managerial opportunity.

Managers and HR Professionals Need to Increase Millennial Social Interaction

While results from the Millennial Motivational Factors survey and related examples demonstrate fun and social interaction as integrated motivators, further discussion of social interaction is warranted.

A Portrait of Millennials: Social Interaction

Millennials do not just want their job to be fun; they want their workplace to be a social organization. The examples of our Contributing Experts, as well as dozens of books, research studies, and recruitment campaigns, all reinforce this accelerating trend. Ron Alsop, writing in *The Trophy Kids Grow Up,* states that "Some companies are helping young employees find opportunities to socialize together both at work and after hours. Such activities build camaraderie as employees get better acquainted with each other and learn about common interests."

Social Interaction and Technology

Much of this part outlines the Millennials' high need for social interaction. However, we cannot overlook the fact that Millennials are described as "growing up digital," with computer games, cell phones, and the Internet as a given.

In *Workforce Crisis*, Dychtwald, Erickson, and Morison state that "For them, technology is not an occasional tool, but a constant extension of themselves. They are accustomed to instant communication and long-distance collaboration. For many purposes, they prefer phone contact, email, or instant messaging to face-to-face communication."

The ability to increase social interaction through technology has enormous potential for the Millennial knowledge worker. In *Generation Blend: Managing Across the Technology Gap,* Rob Salkowitz illustrates how technology and generational differences are on a collision course. However, he also proactively provides solutions to reconciling the best that younger and older workers have to offer. In his discussion of Millennials in the workforce, he makes several points related to technology and the motivational factor of social interaction.

- **Raised to collaborate**

  Millennials have been raised to collaborate. And an ever-expanding constellation of technology (including social networking sites) allows for self expression, instant person-to-person contact, and communal activities around shared interests.

- **Global orientation**

  The Millennials' world is far more expansive than previous generations'. Through online social networks, they can reach beyond the confines of geography to establish relationships with others.

- **Personal networks at work**

  Not only do Millennials require remote access and mobility, but they also require access to personal networks at work.

- **Positive social interactions**

  The technological aspects of Millennial work styles have positive social and organizational implications. Collaboration tools can be used to create cross-disciplinary communities, communities of expertise, and systems to discover new people with whom to collaborate.

Part Three of this book began by identifying Millennials as collaborative by nature, thriving on continuous feedback, supporting open communication, and seeking out social networks. Logically, they also seek out technology-driven communication and collaboration systems, portals, workspaces, and teamware. These tools not only add fun and social interaction to the workplace, but also advance organizational performance.

Fun and Social Interaction: Examples

In this section, several Contributing Experts provide examples of introducing fun and social interaction into the workplace to advance organizational performance.

Fun and Social Interaction at The Urban Institute

Deborah K. Hoover, HR Director
The Urban Institute

Whether it's the annual holiday party, a summer picnic, a softball team, or more serious research-oriented staff activities, Institute staff enjoy interacting with their colleagues. Without question, exit interview responses to the question about "What staff liked best" are resoundingly "the people."

The RAA Discussion Series is a particularly good example of how Millennials have serious fun at work. The discussion series began as an attempt by management to integrate young researchers more into the intellectual life of the Institute. However, over time the discussion series has morphed into a social and learning community that is self-governed and led by the participants. The group, which consists primarily of researchers in their early to late 20s, meets monthly with senior leadership and senior research staff. At these gatherings, junior researchers hear from nationally known experts in their policy fields and have the opportunity to network with the experts and their colleagues from other research programs.

In addition, the group hosts social functions (happy hours, outings in D.C., etc.) and organizes an annual Institutional charitable activity serving the larger D.C. metropolitan community. This group addresses several motivational factors particularly relevant to Millennials. In all, it is a blend of fun, socializing, and learning that speaks to employees across levels as they share ideas, argue policy, and get to know each other as people.

Creating an Enjoyable Work Environment

Kitty Nix, Director, Strategic Development
Helios HR

The following quiz will help you assess your organization's progress in creating a work environment that Millennials are likely to enjoy.

Is Your Workplace Fun?: A Quiz

Select a colleague with whom you work closely and discuss each of the following items. At the end of the discussion, see if you can reach consensus regarding whether your workplace provides a "fun" environment.

	Yes	No
1. Can you think of a time when you saw the CEO or a member of the senior management team laugh?	❑	❑
2. Does your organization have regular social events such as family picnics, holiday parties, or social hours?	❑	❑
3. Do groups of people regularly go out to lunch together?	❑	❑
4. Does your organization publicly recognize individual and team contributions?	❑	❑
5. Does your office have a place for employees to gather informally, such as a break room or lounge?	❑	❑
6. Does your employer encourage employees, including recent hires and junior employees, to generate creative ideas for having fun?	❑	❑
7. Does your organization celebrate individual milestones such as anniversaries, birthdays, weddings, babies, and so forth?	❑	❑
8. Does your company have a regular newsletter that includes humorous articles?	❑	❑

Action Plan: What recommendations can you and your colleague make to increase the fun in your workplace? How would it increase social interaction? Productivity? Retention?

Fun and Social Interaction: Four Examples

Neil Sawyer, Senior Director of Human Resources
The Campagna Center

With many companies experiencing lean times, my experiences with one organization in particular demonstrate the Millennial motivators of fun and social interaction. The organization put together an informal program of social events, excursions, and community outreach initiatives that are low cost and employee driven.

Habitat for Humanity

One program provides paid time off for employees who volunteer for Habitat for Humanity. The initial thought was to give employees incentives to take an active part in an outreach program that is related to our industry. Employees can take hours off or a full day. The company goes a step further by making a matching contribution to Habitat for Humanity. This appeals to many younger employees who are socially conscious and eager to be involved at a grassroots level. Employees are encouraged to make monetary contributions throughout the year with matching funds being given by the company.

Low-Cost Trips and Social Events

This company has held many low-cost trips and social events. Employees are often willing to pay their own way for social events and excursions as long as the planning is done and in place. Weekend day trips to New York or Atlantic City have been very successful. The company rents the tour bus, offers a discounted rate for employees, and provides convenient pickup/drop-off times and places. Employees like the convenience of being able to pay and go.

The value in this strategy is that employees get to do things that they might not do if the planning was entirely their own. The company benefits by the increased interactions between employees who might not have any contact during a workday. It is simple to put together—the company provides the place or means of travel, the employees provide the rest. After years of doing this, we have never had an employee express anything but gratefulness for the generosity of the company for providing the outlet for socializing.

Partnering with Local Businesses

Another way we have brought discounted outings to employees is to partner with local businesses. Newly established businesses are often looking for endorsements from companies with name recognition. In exchange for the right of the business owner to say that our company is a valued customer, he or she will offer (sometimes deep) discounts to our employees. Everything from Paintball excursions to dining to rentals and hotel stays have been discounted to staff on a regular basis. To many of the younger and lower-paid employees, this is a valuable perk of the job.

A Free Day Off

One of our biggest perks comes in the form of a free day off. This day is usually around an established holiday but is not always linked to it. The CEO of the company is the sole determiner of what days they will be. There is seldom any significant advance notice. The CEO will send out an e-mail message about some aspect of life or an amusing story to all staff. At the end of the message, he will tie it into a good reason to take the day off. Employees have come to enjoy his writings as much as having the free day off.

Fun and Social Interaction: From Google to Online Recruiting Company

Christopher R. Ryan, Deputy General Counsel
K12 Inc.

Google's Headquarters and Satellite Offices

The media regularly report on leading work environments that provide amusing and entertaining opportunities for their employees, fueling Millennials' expectations that work will also be fun. Reports on the work environment at Google's headquarters and satellite offices almost sound too good to be true: gourmet cafeterias; not just a foosball table but complete game rooms; relaxation "pods"; on-site masseuses; slides instead of stairwells; a bring-your-pet-to-work policy—these are just a handful of examples.

Unfortunately, most companies aren't as fortunate as Google to have a market capitalization of over $100 billion and over $15 billion in cash on hand. Google also has the advantage of being a technology company that adopted an offbeat and fun culture at the time of its founding, achieved tremendous success very quickly, and managed to maintain its original culture. As a result of Google's unusual situation, it is impossible for companies to simply adopt the Google model; however, there are things that every company can do to foster fun and frivolity.

An Online Recruiting Company

For example, an online recruiting company I worked for cultivated a fun work environment as a way to attract, motivate, and retain its young workforce. A company-sponsored softball team welcomed players of all abilities and held post-game celebrations—win or lose, of course. The kitchen area featured satellite televisions with remote controls. Employees did not spend hours during the day watching their favorite shows, but they did enjoy the brief escape that the television provided as they heated up their lunch in the microwave or took a short break. There was also a foosball room, which was most frequently occupied long after the close of business by software developers who needed a diversion from a long day of coding.

Upon closing a deal, members of the sales department were encouraged to hit a full-size gong that resonated throughout the entire floor to announce their achievement. While a loud gong sound was admittedly a bit distracting at times, it was also an important reminder that the company had obtained a new customer and additional revenue to fuel the company's operations and future growth. Additionally, each department had its own "break out" room that department members designed themselves, within a specified budget.

Despite, or possibly because of, this concentration on fun, the company was very successful and was able to attract a steady stream of new workers as it grew. While a traditional manager or employer might have viewed these fun activities as counterproductive distractions, companies have to adapt to the expectations and work habits of Millennials.

Today's Millennial workers, at least the realistic ones who are in the majority, understand that they cannot expect to work in an environment that is as fun and whimsical as the "Googleplex" (Google even has a fun name for their headquarters building). At the same time, any initiatives that a company can take to inject a little entertainment and amusement into the workplace will satisfy Millennials' expectations for fun and should result in higher job satisfaction, lower attrition rates, and therefore more productivity from this next generation of workers.

Fun and Social Interaction at HireStrategy

Hector Velez, Executive Vice President
HireStrategy

HireStrategy goes beyond the simple balance of the professional and the personal. HireStrategy espouses and acts on a philosophy of not only balance, but integration as well. Our exceedingly dedicated staff members, due to their work ethic and business demands, already make work part of their personal lives. It only makes sense that there is some *quid pro quo*. HireStrategy supports the insertion of employees' personal lives into the workplace. For example, an individual who is "plugged in" 24/7 should have, and does have, the flexibility to leave "early" to attend a child's soccer practice.

In addition to our annual performers club trip to a sunny locale, HireStrategy holds both offsite Annual Kick-Offs and Quarterly Meetings. These meetings include team-by-team reporting on business results, analysis, and plans. But they also include a fun outing. Examples of fun outings range from a day at Dave & Busters to a day at Strike Bethesda. In between, we also have team-building exercises such as "Positive Flooding." Every employee gets an opportunity to hear all of his or her colleagues articulate positive attributes about them!

HireStrategy's annual holiday party includes the employees along with their spouses/partners or significant others. Every party has a different theme. Last year we had a Casino Night, complete with a Pit Boss and croupiers/dealers at the different tables.

Other fun activities include:

- Bagel Wednesdays (free bagels for the staff)
- Monthly all-hands meetings (recognitions of birthdays, HireStrategy anniversaries, and so on)
- Outings to live performances
- Happy hours
- Sports (tag football, softball, etc.)

Most important, "fun" and "social interaction" are not extraneous organizational activities, but are rather a fluent extension of the HireStrategy culture. It is not by accident that employees can be heard saying "This is a great place to work."

Further Discussion

Shira Harrington, Director, Professional Search
Positions, Inc.

Contributing Expert Christopher Ryan aptly notes, "While a traditional manager or employer might have viewed these fun activities as counterproductive distractions, companies have to adapt to the expectations and work habits of Millennials."

This concept of creating a fun workplace to accommodate Millennials can be a source of contention for many older workers, particularly Boomers and Veterans, who don't believe that this type of fun has any place in a serious work environment. Many corporate cultures are not nearly as progressive or Millennial-friendly as Google. In fact, some in corporate America have not even adopted any sort of flexible scheduling, let alone days off for volunteer activities. The challenge for many employers will, again, be overcoming old mindsets with relation to incorporating fun into the workplace.

Many Boomer (and even older Gen X) managers struggle with the seemingly ongoing social interactions that many Millennials engage in throughout the day. What was once the occasional "water-cooler talk" for older workers has become an elongated social bonding between Millennials that can cause their managers to believe (rightly or wrongly) that work is simply not getting done.

Although for many Millennials, work and social interaction are one and the same, perception can be reality when it comes to performance management. How do employers change the mindsets of seasoned professionals when it comes to *how* and *when* work gets done? How do we truly move beyond face time and allow Millennials needed fun time in the workplace?

Summary

This part focused on four key points. First, fun and social interaction are significant motivational factors that must be acknowledged and valued as human capital assets. Second, managers and human resources professionals must incorporate strategies to integrate fun in the workplace. Third, opportunities for incorporating technology- and non-technology-based social interaction strategies must also be incorporated into the workplace. Finally, Contributing Experts provided a variety of examples of how fun and social interaction meet Millennial motivational needs.

The authors of *Workforce Crisis* state, "What many young people need most to feel happy in a company is the continuous opportunity to learn and grow through frequent changes in roles, responsibilities, and programs." The opportunity to work for an organization that reflects their personal values and beliefs provides a variety of platforms to make a significant contribution and is almost an extension of their need for on-the-job fun and social interaction.

PART 4

Purpose, Contribution, and Challenging Work

> ***"Generation Y employees [Millennials] bring specific values and ideals to the business world that ultimately will alter workplace policies and management strategies. Companies that make an effort to understand and act upon these professionals' viewpoints will find themselves with a dedicated and ambitious group of workers."***
>
> –**from *What Millennial Workers Want: How to Attract and Retain Gen Y Employees***

In this part:

- Getting Started
- New Rules for Employment: Placing Millennials in Perspective
- The Millennials' Need to Make and Be Recognized for their Contributions
- The Manager's Role in Motivating Millennials as Contributors
- Challenging Work: Global, National, and Organizational Issues

Getting Started

As with previous parts of this book, this part is driven by our survey of Millennial motivational factors. Responses that are relevant to this part include the value Millennials place on "purpose," "contribution," "challenging work," "passion for work," "fast cycle work environment," "accomplishment," and "pride in work environment." After analyzing the data, we combined similar factors. Since "purpose," "contribution," and "challenging work" appeared in the top eleven frequencies of responses and are closely interrelated as motivational factors, they were combined and emerged as Part Four: Purpose, Contribution, and Challenging Work.

Common themes that appear in a variety of Millennial books, research studies, and the workplace are the Millennials' sense of purpose, the desire to contribute, and the need for challenging work. For a variety of reasons, Millennials begin work by setting tremendous goals for themselves. As Cam Marston states in *Motivating the "What's in it for Me?" Workforce*, "They know what they want to do and where they want to be." He goes on to say, "They have no idea how to get there, mostly because they lack sufficient experience to create the blueprint that will get them from where they are today to their goals. And that is where their bosses come into the picture."

Cam Marston's statement reinforces the objectives of this part. Helping the Millennial knowledge worker to find purpose, opportunities to contribute, and challenging work is a shared, collaborative responsibility of the Millennial, the manager, and the organization. This premise drives the objectives of this part:

- Recognize that Millennials have a strong sense of purpose that drives their careers and lives. They expect their employer to provide flexible opportunities to meet this need.
- Acknowledge that Millennials have a profound need to be recognized for the contributions they make to their workplaces and society.
- Understand that Millennial knowledge workers are high-achieving multitaskers requiring a variety of challenging assignments and projects.

New Rules for Employment: Placing Millennials in Perspective

The challenge of motivating Millennial knowledge workers is significantly influenced by a trend that started well over a decade ago. It has been exacerbated by current economic conditions, requiring organizations to reinvent themselves in order to address a global economic crisis.

More specifically, William Bridges wrote, as far back as 1994, that "the old rules [of employment] are gone. Finished. Disappeared and left no forwarding address." These "old rules," which, fortunately, Millennials and Gen Xers have little knowledge of, were built on the following four-point paradigm. Quoting Bridges directly (from *JobShift*):

> “ ***Yesterday's organizations, built on the job paradigm,***
>
> — ***'located' the employee at a particular level on a vertical hierarchy, responsible to the person above and responsible for the people (if any) below;***
>
> — ***'located' the employee horizontally, as well, in a department or functional unit that was responsible for some particular kind of work, for example, engineering, accounting, or sales;***
>
> — ***gave each employee a well-defined area of responsibility, which was formalized in a job description;***
>
> — ***laid out before ambitious employees "career paths" that they could aspire to follow upward through the hierarchy … —a stepping-stone path of jobs toward greater power and financial reward.***

As previously stated, these old rules are gone. Interestingly, the "new rules" for employment, outlined by Bridges in 1994, are remarkably similar to the Millennial knowledge workers' need for their organizations to help them find a sense of purpose through flexible employment opportunities and work assignments. The following organizational assessment is based on material appearing in *JobShift*.

NEW RULES FOR EMPLOYMENT AND MILLENNIAL MOTIVATIONAL NEEDS

Review each of the following statements and identify those strategies and tactics your organization currently embraces in support of the motivation factor of purpose. Also, identify those that need more attention.

New Employment Rules	Currently Supports	Needs Attention
1. Everyone is a contingent worker. Everyone's employment is contingent on the results the organization can achieve.	❑	❑
2. Recognizing the turbulence in the business environment, Millennials need to regard themselves as people whose value to the organization must be demonstrated in each successive situation they find themselves in.	❑	❑
3. Workers need to develop a mindset, and a way of managing their own careers, that is more like an external vendor than like a traditional employee.	❑	❑
4. Companies will work with these new-style workers collaboratively to make the relationship as mutually beneficial as possible.	❑	❑
5. Workers must be able to switch their focus rapidly from one task to another, to work in situations where the group is the responsible party and the manager only a coordinator, to work without clear-cut job descriptions, and to work on several projects at a time.	❑	❑
6. Ultimately, it is the Millennials who must manage their careers and lives.	❑	❑

As a result of completing the previous assessment, I have identified the following strategy to utilize the motivational factor of Purpose:

____

____

____

Reconciling Millennials' and Managers' Expectations

For the purpose of this part, the Millennial motivational factors of purpose, contributions, and challenging work are treated separately. This approach allows for the presentation of a broad variety of strategies and examples. However, in reality, managers and human resources professionals will find that they will be required to address all three motivational factors concurrently.

Millennials' Purpose Expectations

- Work that is personally stimulating
- Work that makes a true impact on social issues, the environment, labor standards, globalization, diversity, and corporate citizenship
- Work that is of demonstrable value to their organization, clients, and community

Managers' Purpose Expectations and Strategies

- Manage Millennials' expectations in a way that pays off for both employee and employer
- Show new hires how their work makes a difference and why it is valuable to the organization
- Offer a rich variety of opportunities to advance their careers
- As a boss, inspire Millennials in their work and lead them
- Engage in the types and frequency of communication that Millennials prefer
- Provide challenging work that is purposeful and really matters
- Ensure that Millennials know why they are doing whatever it is they are doing
- Communication "just in time" and "all the time"

Communicating Purpose

The previous discussion works with the assumption that Millennial knowledge workers have a desire to do purposeful work and to make a significant contribution to their organization and, most often, society. A recurring theme in reconciling Millennial and manager expectations is the mutual responsibility to collaborate and communicate. Contributing Expert Sue McLeod of Hay Group takes these concepts a step further in sharing the importance of leadership style as a strategy to communication purpose.

Practice What You Preach

Sue McLeod, Senior Consultant
Hay Group

Hay Group's research into effective leaders shows that there are six basic leadership styles, and successful leaders use them all—in the right situation.

The younger generation's desire to do purposeful work and to make significant contributions requires their leaders and managers to use a Visionary Leadership style. You're using the Visionary Leadership style when you:

- Communicate your organization's goals, mission, and strategy, including the contribution to your customers and society.
- Explain why a project, job, or task is important to achieving the mission.
- Remind employees how their contributions (no matter how small) make a difference to the organization, the customer, and their colleagues.

There are also styles that will diminish employee engagement over time, especially with employees who want to understand their purpose and feel like part of the team. Be careful if you find yourself using the Directive style, which is focused on immediate compliance, uses "directives" (often referred to as the "command and control" style), and motivates with the threat of negative consequences. You're using the Directive style when you:

- Tell employees what to do and how to do it.
- Finish your instructions (either out loud or in your head) with some variation of "Or else…."
- Answer "Why?" with some variation of "Because I said so."
- Closely monitor your employees, ready to give another directive (or threat) if they deviate from the defined task.

The Millennials' Need to Make and Be Recognized for their Contributions

In *Millennials Rising: The Next Great Generation*, Neil Howe and William Strauss state, "The Millennial future is what America is destined to become—and soon… With Millennials rising, America needs to start thinking bigger. Test them. Challenge them. Put difficult tasks before them, and have faith that they can do themselves and their nation proud." This enthusiastic statement, made in 2000, has become today's reality. And it is not a coincidence that the Motivational Factors Survey resulted in "Contributions" being ranked high on the list. Perhaps the most effective way to discuss the motivational factor of contribution is to view it through the twin lenses of Millennial and manager.

Millennials as Visionary Contributors

Rob Salkowitz's recent book *Generation Blend* captures the ultimate power of the Millennials' potential contribution to the workplace in Chapter Eight, titled "Ambassadors of the Future: Turning to Younger Workers for Strategic Insights." He begins and ends the chapter with research-based statements that I am taking the liberty of reformatting as a "Declaration of Intent."

THE POTENTIAL OF THE MILLENNIALS' CONTRIBUTION: A DECLARATION OF INTENT

Of the following statements, select the one that best reflects your belief in the contributions that Millennials can make.

____ 1. "When Millennials hit the workforce in significant numbers, they are going to shake things up. They are the blue-chip prospects organizations will look to for new energy, new ideas, and titanic productivity."

____ 2. "With their numbers, their collective purpose, and their global perspective, they can't help but transform the workplace and the world."

____ 3. "Organizations that have the right investments in place to capitalize on the skills and work styles of Millennials … will be best positioned to unleash their vast creative and productive potential."

____ 4. "Connected, self-aware, and sophisticated Millennials are often particularly perceptive and articulate when given the opportunity to focus on issues that are important to them."

____ 5. "[T]he organizational commitment to engage with Millennials as partners in the formation of a strategic vision can be as valuable as the direct knowledge gained from the engagement."

There is no doubt that Millennials bring a set of very special strengths to the workplace. They are, as the previous statements suggest, adaptable, creative, independent thinkers, and quick learners. And they seek opportunities to contribute right away. With this appreciation of the rich contributions that Millennials can make, the question to answer is how managers motivate and engage Millennials so they actually contribute.

Millennials as Contributing Leaders

As many of our reader/practitioners know, you do not have to be a manager to be a leader. In fact, many Millennials would suggest that their manager might not be a leader. At the same time, as there is increasingly greater professionalization of the workforce—knowledge workers—and a corresponding flattening of organizational management levels, there is a tremendous opportunity for Millennials to emerge as leaders. This is what Jennell Evans, Contributing Expert, describes in the following example.

The Emerging Leaders Institute

Jennell Evans, President and CEO
Strategic Interactions

In addition to contributing to their employers' goals, Millennials seek opportunities to serve in their community, which connects to their desire for work/life balance. A great example of this is the overwhelming successful Emerging Leaders Institute, an initiative of Leadership Fairfax, Inc., headquartered near Tyson's Corner, Virginia.

Founded in 2003, the Emerging Leaders Institute (ELI) is an application-based program that brings together participants from all kinds of private, public, and nonprofit sectors in the Washington D.C. metro area. This nine-month program, dedicated to "inspiring, developing, and connecting young community leaders," provides opportunities for hands-on community service projects like renovating group homes or organizing food banks.

Relationships are forged through shared experiences such as group skills training, community service projects, and preparation to serve on nonprofit boards. Millennials get to see the impact of their community service work and see how they can make a difference in their own backyards.

The program has built-in feedback (Millennials love this!), with coaches and a mentor (usually a Leadership Fairfax Institute alum) assigned to each person attending the program.

Another cornerstone of the program is leadership skills training. Millennials tend to seek more responsibility and leadership opportunities earlier in their careers than did previous generations. As participants in the ELI program, they learn critical communication skills such as conflict management and negotiating.

The Manager's Role in Motivating Millennials as Contributors

There are no shortcuts to effectively manage others regardless of the generation of manager or employee. In essence, "being a good manager" means "being a good manager." But as the authors of *What Millennial Workers Want: How to Attract and Retain Gen Y Employees* state, "[F]or Millennials, having a good boss is particularly important. This is a group that has high expectations for authority figures and craves continued feedback and reinforcement. Pairing these staff members with your best managers will go a long way toward keeping these employees satisfied and productive."

Before examining specific strategies and tactics that managers can employ to maximize the contribution they make to an organization, an opportunity is presented for you to assess yourself as a Millennial "dream boss." The following assessment is based on *What Millennial Workers Want: How to Attract and Retain Gen Y Employees*, a report of survey findings by Robert Half International and Yahoo! HotJobs.

A Millennial's Portrait of a Dream Boss: A Self-Assessment

Indicate your greatest strengths and areas requiring further development. Share the results of this self-assessment with a colleague and staff member and seek feedback. Are your views of your strengths and areas to improve in concurrence with your colleague's or staff's feedback? If you want to go for bonus points, ask your Millennials to provide their feedback.

Current Strength	Future Goal	Aspects of a Dream Boss
❑	❑	Skillful manager, advisor, and supporter
❑	❑	Pleasant and easy to get along with
❑	❑	Understanding and caring
❑	❑	Flexible and open-minded
❑	❑	Respects/values/appreciates employees
❑	❑	Good communication skills

Motivating Millennials as Contributors by Understanding Millennials as Contributors

Ken Blanchard, whom you may know as the originator of the concept of the One-Minute Manager, once stated that "What motivates people is what motivates people." Building on his riddle-like statement, we can say, "Motivating Millennials as contributors begins by understanding Millennials as contributors." This requires that we understand Millennials as both Millennials and knowledge workers.

The behaviors and characteristics of the four generational groups have been influenced by a variety of events and environmental factors. This has led to the methodology of generational analysis. Since the 1991 publication of William Strauss and Neil Howe's book *Generations*, there has emerged a methodology for attracting, recruiting, managing, motivating, and retaining Millennials. While I personally agree with Contributing Expert Rick Humphress that this may be a simplification of a way to understand human behavior, the concept of generational analysis does provide a basic frame of reference.

With this concept of generational analysis as an acceptable methodology, we can move forward and describe several of the behavioral characteristics of Millennials as contributors. Lisa Orrell writes in *Millennials Incorporated*, "Although the Millennial Generation is said to be the brightest and best educated generation our country has ever seen, and even though they typically far surpass their Gen X and Boomer bosses and co-workers in the area of being tech-savvy, this unique group of young adults certainly isn't arriving to the professional world without their fair share of 'baggage.'"

Millennials as Contributors: Challenges and Strategies for the Manager

Select a challenge that you face to further maximize your Millennials' contributions. Then select one or more managerial strategies to motivate Millennials and maximize their contributions.

Behavioral Challenges

____ 1. While very independent and bright, Millennials need to be given a clear path and a plan for accomplishing a task.

____ 2. They are willing to work hard and make creative contributions while "on the job," but want respect for their time outside of work with friends, family, and interests.

____ 3. There is no doubt that Millennials are goal oriented and highly productive. However, they want to know the reason for a delegation or assignment and its ultimate goal.

____ 4. They want to be free to ask questions and to share their feelings and ideas, and they want constant feedback and recognition for their contributions.

Managerial Strategies

____ 1. Establish a communication environment, in informal hallway conversations, before meetings, and during meetings, that encourages participation and contribution.

____ 2. Consider, as mentioned earlier in the book, the power of the environment. Provide open and informal spaces for collaborative engagement.

____ 3. Create a culture of continuous learning, introduction of new ideas, and a variety of assignments that provide opportunities to encourage contribution.

____ 4. Challenge and delegate nonstop. As Lisa Orrell writes, "They want to make a difference and have an unlimited capacity to contribute."

Opportunities to maximize Millennial contributions are unlimited. However, as Contributing Expert Rick Humphress previously pointed out, we must be cautious in using generations as the single differentiator of behavior. He reminds us that on an individual level, one Millennial can be quite different from another. Nonetheless, we can generalize, based on research, that Millennial knowledge workers are entrepreneurial hard workers who are techno-savvy and thrive on flexibility.

Organizations, managers, and human resources professionals can maximize Millennial contributions by customizing work responsibilities, designing flexible and responsive career paths, and providing education and training opportunities. Maximizing Millennial contributions depends on being able to answer the questions that Millennials typically ask, as presented in *Managing Generation Y*:

- What value can I add today?
- What can I learn today?
- What will you offer me today?
- How will I be rewarded today?

Understanding Millennials as Knowledge Workers

In the broadest sense, Millennials are defined by anchor years that identify an age cohort ranging from 19 to 30 years of age. As discussed earlier in the book, different researchers differ slightly in defining the age range. However, the focus of this book is not on Millennials who can work in a variety of service, manufacturing, or technology industries. This book focuses on Millennial knowledge workers, who are defined by Frances Horibe as those "who [use their] head more than their hands to produce value" and most likely are college educated.

In order to maximize the Millennials' contributions to the workplace, one must also understand this Millennial knowledge worker. This group includes a broader population than just computer programmers. As Frances Horibe writes in *Managing Knowledge Workers*, "knowledge workers are not just employees in high-tech companies. People in advertising agencies, consulting companies, financial institutions—anyone who uses their head more than their hands to create wealth—are all knowledge workers." From this perspective, then, it's clear that additional strategies are needed.

Consultation and Involvement: Strategies for Engagement

In order to maximize the hard-working, achievement-oriented attributes of Millennial knowledge workers, organizations must embrace strategies of consultation and involvement to increase engagement. Following is a brief explanation of each strategy and its advantages, and an application exercise.

Engagement Strategy One: The Consultation Process

In *Managing Knowledge Workers*, Frances Horibe provides us with a formal definition of the consultation process and the advantages of using it as a strategy to heighten knowledge workers' contributions:

> ***"Consultation is a process by which management seeks the opinion of employees on important issues of the day. It is primarily about testing the waters since, with consultation, the right to decide the issue is with management. Consulting allows employees to express an opinion about their future."***

According to Horibe, the following are the advantages of using the consultative strategy to increase contribution:

- Employees will contribute their intellectual capital only if they believe their opinion counts.
- One way to show employees that their opinions matter is to consult them on corporate issues.
- Issues on which employees are consulted must be both substantive and amenable to influence.
- Employees must understand that they are being consulted, not asked to approve a decision, and that a consensus is not necessary.

THE CONSULTATION PROCESS: AN APPLICATION OPPORTUNITY

1. Does a consultation strategy appear relevant to increasing your Millennial knowledge workers' contributions?
2. If so, indicate how you apply it.

   Specific individual ____________________

   Corporate issue ____________________

   When used ____________________

   How implemented ____________________

   Anticipated outcome ____________________

Engagement Strategy Two: Involvement

Frances Horibe introduces another strategy to increase knowledge worker contributions by tapping the organization's intellectual capital through involvement. A definition of involvement, a list of advantages of using it, and another application opportunity follow.

The involvement process is a strategy that asks individuals to decide or recommend on major challenges. "Not only will this approach bring to light more of the implicit knowledge people have of what might work, [but] it will also challenge their creativity and reinforce their belief that you value their opinions and knowledge" (Horibe). As a reader/practitioner, you can appreciate this strategy's potential to increase the Millennial knowledge worker's contributions.

According to Horibe, the following are the advantages of using the involvement strategy to increase contributions:

- Involvement will increase knowledge workers' commitment to the organization, though it will take some time.
- It demonstrates that the employees' opinions count.
- To help the process, a person should be appointed to challenge a function, and all team members should be briefed on the complexities of the issues they are tackling and be trained on how to work as a team.
- While this process doesn't necessarily produce better decisions, it does produce ones to which employees are more committed.

INVOLVEMENT: AN APPLICATION OPPORTUNITY

1. Does an involvement strategy appear relevant to increasing your Millennial knowledge workers' contributions?
2. If so, indicate how you apply it.

Specific individual ______________________________

Corporate issue ______________________________

When used ______________________________

How implemented ______________________________

Anticipated outcome ______________________________

Both the consultation and involvement strategies have the potential to increase the employee's engagement in the workplace. Each strategy has its own advantage. However, as Horibe states, "Involvement changes not merely how work is accomplished, but how completely the heart and brain are involved in the company's business." This is clearly a motivational factor.

Structure, Direction, and Deadlines

There is no doubt that understanding Millennials as contributors and engaging them through consultation and involvement strategies can motivate them. The previously presented strategies provide an opportunity to show that their work makes a difference and is of value to the organization. In addition, it provides an opportunity for the Millennial knowledge worker to participate in work that is stimulating and challenging. And finally, the use of these strategies demonstrates that their work clearly benefits internal and external customers and at times even the community at large.

However, there is also a potential challenge in employing these strategies with Millennials. Research indicates that Millennials require structure and supervision. A review of Millennial research results in the following recommendations.

- Millennials require "regular checking in" by their supervisors to assist with obstacles, answer questions, and to provide guidance.
- Millennial professionals ask "why?" a lot. They want to know a reason for the request, the purpose, and the ultimate goal.
- Nothing should be assumed. Lay out the big picture in clear terms.
- Millennials require careful handling when their performance is not up to par.
- Managers need to provide Millennials with an unusual amount of handholding, reminding them of project deadlines.

In an effort to maximize the Millennials' contributions to the workplace, they need structure and explicit direction. The recommendation to give them a checklist and then be sure that they get the job done appears in a variety of books and studies.

Managers also need to provide specific and frequent clarification of project deadlines. Millennials require encouragement to take some chances and learn from their inevitable mistakes. Finally, managers can teach Millennials to break problems into more manageable units and determine which data are most relevant to the solution.

The manager who recognizes the Millennials' need for structure, direction, deadlines, and clarity can meet not only individual needs, but also organizational needs.

Challenging Work: Global, National, and Organizational Issues

Recent events dramatize a problem far more critical than simply addressing the need to provide Millennials with challenging work. *Workforce 2020: Work and Workers in the 21st Century*, published by the Hudson Institute over a decade ago, predicted the global and national economic challenges we are now facing. It emphasizes the following three principles—not just for motivating Millennials, but for America to maintain its position in a fiercely competitive global economy:

- "The journey to Workforce 2020 is a journey to an uncertain destination. "
- "America must adapt the institutions shaping its labor force to new circumstances. We cannot produce twenty-first-century knowledge workers in nineteenth-century public schools, early-twentieth-century higher education institutions, or mid-twentieth-century federal job training programs."
- "Society-wide solutions will not address America's workforce challenges adequately. … Individual and local experimentation is the order of the day to provide competition in some instances and increase knowledge in others."

Creating a 21st-Century Workplace

Those of us who see the Millennials as the hero generation that will help lead us forward as knowledge workers and become a new breed of leaders recognize that the ultimate and more inclusive solution to creating a twenty-first-century workforce is, as Cam Marston writes in *Motivating the "What's In It For Me?" Workforce,* the need for our organizations to become "fast, functional, and multigenerational." Marston makes a simple, and most critical, point in stating that "Age diversity among employees will be a thorny issue for the foreseeable future. … You'd like to know how to get consistently high performance from *all* your employees." While space does not allow the necessary discussion of a four-generation workforce, the following steps are worth reviewing.

From *Motivating the "What's In It For Me?" Workforce,* here are the four steps for maximizing the productivity of a multigenerational workforce:

1. Identify the problem areas.
2. Rate your success in hiring the best talent.
3. Now that you've got them, learn how to keep your Gen X and new Millennial employees. (Related fact: According to the Bureau of Labor Statistics, the average mid-twenties employee leaves his or her job every 1.3 years.)
4. Spend time getting to know your employees.

Meeting the Contribution Needs of Millennials

Motivating the Millennial Knowledge Worker places emphasis on providing the reader/practitioner with relevant motivational strategies and tactics. This part concludes by presenting recommendations from Contributing Experts.

Provide Challenging Work that Really Matters

Those organizations that want to become a Millennial "employer of choice" must recognize that Millennials have well-documented workplace expectations. And number one, according to *Managing Generation Y* by Carolyn A. Martin, Ph.D. and Bruce Tulgan, is providing challenging work that really matters. Completing the following exercise will provide you with an opportunity to assess your organization's effectiveness in meeting this Millennial expectation.

ORGANIZATIONAL ASSESSMENT

Identify your current organizational strengths and areas for further improvement.

Current Strength	Can Improve	Contribution Opportunity
☐	☐	Educate your young workforce not only about the contributions your products and services make to society, but also about how your organization supports the local community.
☐	☐	Ensure that young workers know why they are doing what they are doing.
☐	☐	Offer team members opportunities to be problem-solvers and innovators by asking them at every team meeting: ▶ What are you doing well? ▶ What are you not doing so well? ▶ How can we do this better?
☐	☐	Throw "creativity parties" where people can socialize, have fun, and brainstorm solutions to a problem the team or organization is facing.
☐	☐	Give young people who earn it the opportunity to take on more challenging liaison, supervision, and project leader roles.

Provide Meaningful Work and Engage Workers

The authors of *Workforce Crisis: How to Beat the Coming Shortage of Skills and Talents* present a fascinating recommendation that is especially relevant to motivating the Millennial knowledge worker. They suggest that "You can completely overhaul the 'employment deal' to provide flexible work arrangements, learning opportunities, and compensation and benefits, but your best employees will still leave if their work neither stimulates them nor brings out their best talents."

While common characteristics of "interesting work" are relevant to all generations, they are specifically important to the Millennial knowledge worker. I have taken the liberty of paraphrasing material that appears in *Workforce Crisis* to create the following Millennial Inventory.

DO I FIND MY WORK INTERESTING? A MILLENNIAL'S PERSPECTIVE

Consider distributing and discussing this exercise at your next one-on-one Millennial mentor meeting. Identify ways you can make improvements.

I find that my work provides opportunities for:

Yes	No	Sources of Interest
☐	☐	Stimulation
☐	☐	Variety
☐	☐	Edification
☐	☐	Increasing connections
☐	☐	Control
☐	☐	Value

Next, the supervisor discusses the following question with a Millennial.

My work would be more interesting if my supervisor:

____

____

____

____

Enhancing the Contribution of Senior Research Staff

Deborah Hoover
The Urban Institute

Millennial researchers often want opportunities to step out from behind those with more experience and to choose for themselves the work relationships and projects that meet their own needs for a sense of purpose and challenging work. Senior research staff can no longer simply lay out all of the design elements of a research project and then task Millennials without consideration of their wants and needs, because they just will not stand for it.

Millennials ask why things matter, why we don't do things differently, and suggest (sometimes quite strongly) alternative approaches. They are far less hesitant to turn down an assignment if they don't see it as a "true opportunity," and they simply quit if they don't see their needs being met. Whereas other employees may see some assignments as the "dues that must be paid," Millennials often decline assignments that don't meet their own personal needs and seek out those that do—even in circumstances in which management is unsupportive and/or punitive.

Managers and supervisors who link work with a sense of purpose, and challenge these bright young people early on, are clearly the most successful in terms of recruitment and retention. Unfortunately, some supervisors simply don't get it. A case in point is illustrated next:

Exit Interview

Audrey was a fabulous researcher; she was extremely accomplished, well connected, and passionate about her work and that of her staff. She recruited only the best and the brightest young researchers, but she just could not keep them. The complaints started as "grapevine" gossip and over time evolved into a dull roar. Exit interview comments include the following:

"I wanted more responsibility, more contact from my boss, and I was bored."

"The general environment—there are a lot of smart, nice people here, but not enough opportunities to bring it out of them."

"I don't feel like I'm having an impact."

And yet, in other parts of the organization, it's clear that supervisors can and do make a huge difference when they understand and work with Millennials in the ways that appeal to them:

"I was trusted with the work and given a lot of responsibility from the beginning."

"I liked the freedom I got, even at the lower level, in terms of pursuing the job I loved doing and the respect I received, even as a new employee."

Enhancing the Contribution of the Financial Services Investment Department

Kris T. Jensen, Vice President, Corporate Services
Wisdom Workers

Faced with the task of retaining and challenging administrative employees, the management team in the investment department of a global financial services giant created self-directed support teams for hundreds of real estate underwriters and investment executives. Team members were carefully selected for their willingness to make decisions, collaborate, and communicate effectively, along with their attention to detail and quality orientation.

While most employees were young and were not college graduates, older long-term employees also became part of the teams, though not always in the team leader role. Employees who were concerned about their ability or desire to work in a participative, self-directed structure were re-assigned to other areas of the company.

To align all the work groups to execute business strategies effectively, we gave each team extensive training to help them understand each other's work styles and learn how to collaborate without management intervention. Because investment employees were located on four floors, a team of service and support employees was assigned to each floor and given budget and service authority to perform on behalf of their internal "clients."

All four teams also had to coordinate assignments from one floor to another in order to keep their workloads even; e.g., when a team on one floor had more work than they could process, they could use the other three teams to supplement their staff. The teams had to negotiate and renegotiate their own clients' priorities, along with assisting a sister team.

Under the direction of the senior manager, who was ultimately responsible for the entire service system, team members participated in hiring and firing as well as in providing individual employee performance feedback. All employees were held accountable for problem solving, production, and innovation, consulting with the senior manager only when they could not identify an optimal solution or service offering.

Management focused on establishing and maintaining a work environment that assured competent teams, along with creating communication processes for regular debriefings, information exchange, and mediation processes when the teams ran into disputes they couldn't resolve themselves.

Because employees had tremendous control over their work and participated in key operational decisions while being highly accountable for products and services, this team structure allowed management to recruit and retain high-performing multigenerational employees with no turnover. Additionally, fewer than 30 employees could support more than 500 professionals.

Enhancing Contributions of Registered Nurses

Lesley Channell, Assistant Vice President of Human Resources
Dominion Hospital and Reston Hospital Center

Healthcare is not immune from having a workforce comprising four generations of workers. Over the years, there has been a lot of discussion about not "eating our young" when it comes to the orientation of new Registered Nurses. In-services on this topic have been given to our Nursing Directors and are incorporated in our Charge Nurse workshop in an effort to embrace all ages of workers. The level of technology proficiency is very high for the 21–30-year-old workers. They are very easy to train, but the Nursing Directors have noticed that these workers need a lot of reassurance and praise on a frequent basis.

The Director must be two steps ahead of young workers, thinking of projects to keep them engaged because they can become easily bored. This age group is constantly looking at ways to fix and upgrade processes. We know that an employee who has a friend at work is usually a more engaged employee. This group seems to require friends at work, versus other age groups that see that as a nicety. Working in groups provides a better work environment for them than does working alone. This group prefers a collaborative approach to working with physicians and other members of the healthcare provider team.

New grad RNs don't view being a nurse as the final destination of their career path. They typically don't want to "just be a nurse," so they are focused on obtaining a masters degree and becoming certified in their field. However, climbing the ladder cannot occur at the expense of an imbalance between work and life needs.

Further Discussion

Shira Harrington, Director, Professional Search Positions, Inc.

Jennell Evans made an excellent comment about Millennials when she aptly wrote, "As participants in the Emerging Leader Program, they learn critical communication skills such as conflict management and negotiating." Many Millennials, having been raised by doting parents who showered, and continue to shower, frequent praise on their children, are not accustomed either to receiving constructive—let alone outright negative—feedback from their bosses or to dealing with interpersonal conflicts.

In addition, with the advent of Internet search engines, many Millennials believe that if the researched information is not on Google, it must not exist. (Robert Wendover, President of Generation Trends, calls this phenomenon "menu-driven thinking," referring to the drop-down menus used in the Help function of software programs.) This, along with the trend of most Millennials having been raised in team environments, both in school and in extracurricular activities, has led to a lack of individual problem-solving abilities and strategic thinking. This is notwithstanding that they are still young and relatively inexperienced.

As a result of these variables, employers should make a concerted effort to create challenging work assignments not only to appeal to Millennials' desire for stimulating and creative work but also to purposely mentor them in resolving conflicts and thinking strategically. Future discussions should be had around specific strategies to engage and train Millennials in these two areas, because they have been socialized in such a way as to be significantly lacking in these skills, more so than other generations.

Summary

Part Four's objectives focused on three key points. First, Millennials have a strong sense of purpose that drives their careers and lives. They expect their employer to provide flexible opportunities to meet this need. Second, Millennials have a profound need to make and be recognized for the contributions they make to their workplaces and to society. And third, Millennial knowledge workers tend to be high-achieving multitaskers who require a variety of challenging assignments.

From Part Four: Purpose, Contribution, and Challenging Work, we move on to Part Five: Establishing and Sustaining Effective Communication. The manager who demonstrates the ability to understand and respond to the Millennials' communication expectations will find that he or she is also reinforcing and recognizing the importance that Millennials place on purpose, contribution, and challenging work.

PART 5

Establishing and Sustaining Effective Communication

> ***"One of the most profound impacts of networked information and communication technology is the way it reduces—and potentially eliminates—the need for concepts such as the workplace and the workday." "The ability to manage in this kind of information-rich environment is often cited as one of the critical differences in generational workstyles."***
>
> ***–Generation Blend: Managing Across the Technology Age Gap***

In this part:

- Getting Started
- The Importance of Establishing and Sustaining Effective Communication
- Strategies and Tactics
- Collaboration Technologies

Getting Started

As with previous parts of this book, this part is driven by our survey of Millennial motivational factors. Responses that are relevant to this part include "understanding," "treatment as colleagues," "interest in employees," "humor," "communication all the time," and "frequent feedback." Similar descriptors of motivational factors were combined, and Part Five, Establish and Sustain Effective Communication, emerged.

Further research and Contributing Experts' recommendations resulted in this part's focus on the following four objectives:

- Review the "Portrait of a Millennial" (in this book's Introduction) to reinforce the importance of establishing and sustaining effective communication.
- Acknowledge that establishing effective communication is a shared responsibility of Millennial and manager.
- Identify strategies and tactics that managers can use to establish and sustain effective communication with Millennials.
- Understand why collaborative technologies are not only promising new information tools for the enterprise, but a critical communication tool for Millennials who are highly networked on and off the job.

The Importance of Establishing and Sustaining Effective Communication

The "Portrait of a Millennial" (in this book's Introduction) is relevant as we discuss the motivational factor of establishing and sustaining effective communication. Integrating what has been described as the most demanding and coddled generation in history into the workplace is a challenge. To what degree their behavior has been shaped by the driven Baby Boomer generation, new Web 2.0 technologies, and an unpredictable and volatile global economy are all moot points.

What is relevant is an understanding of a collective portrait of Millennials as it relates to communication. The following Millennial Communication Portrait is presented as a frame of reference for this part.

MILLENNIAL COMMUNICATION PORTRAIT: 13 KEY BEHAVIORS

Select those behaviors that influence your ability to establish and sustain effective communication with Millennials.

____ 1. Millennials are trusting of their parents and other authority figures.

____ 2. Millennials are team-oriented, confident, and optimistic.

____ 3. They are a highly networked and connected generation.

____ 4. They are accustomed to receiving recognition for practically every achievement, no matter how trivial.

____ 5. They expect to be treated as special and receive constant feedback.

____ 6. Their self-esteem is most important.

____ 7. They require a comfortable, low-stress environment.

____ 8. They appreciate a manager who has a sense of humor.

____ 9. They want to respect their manager and in turn be respected.

____ 10. They desire consistent mentoring and constructive feedback.

____ 11. They are inclusive by nature.

____ 12. The content of communication is less important than the act of communicating.

____ 13. They are eager to please.

Identify those unique Millennial behaviors that you need to give further consideration in an effort to establish and sustain effective communication.

Establishing and Sustaining Effective Communication is a Shared Responsibility of Manager and Millennial

There are two major reasons that communication, negotiation, motivation, and other competency strategies often fail. First, a manager may diligently initiate an effective strategy in an effort to improve the manager/employee relationship and assume that this is all that is needed. Wrong. What is needed is ongoing and varied follow-up to sustain and support the process. Second, communication is not thought of as a shared responsibility between two individuals, most often a manager and an employee. With this shared-responsibility concept in mind, let us now take a look at the Millennials' and managers' communication needs and responsibilities.

Millennials' Communication Expectations and Responsibilities

Millennials have been described as a self-reliant generation comfortable with themselves and others. Jean M. Twenge, author of *Generation Me,* also describes them as confident, assertive, and entitled. She labels them as "Generation Direct." The following quote from her book sets the scene for our next point.

> ***"Some older business managers complain that young people are too blunt. These managers say that young employees ask for instant feedback that's straightforward and uncomplicated, and give it in return. Some managers are surprised at young people's willingness to critique the performance of older workers."***
>
> **–Jean M. Twenge**

The implications of Generation Direct's communication preferences have a clear impact on the discussion, in *What Millennial Workers Want: How to Attract and Retain Gen Y Employees,* of the Millennials' perspective on "The Boss Factor" and "The Coworker Factor." Let us begin with "The Boss Factor."

The Boss Factor and Millennial Communication Expectations

Millennials are accustomed to direct, ongoing supervision from parents, teachers, and other authority figures. They seek a similar relationship with their bosses, looking to them for constant feedback.

The following exercises are based on *What Millennial Workers Want: How to Attract and Retain Gen Y Employees*, a report by Robert Half International and Yahoo! HotJobs.

The Boss Factor: A Manager's Self-Assessment

Evaluate your strengths and any areas that require further development. Also consider distributing this form to your Millennials and seeking their feedback.

Are you…	Yes	No
1. A skillful manager, advisor, and supporter?	☐	☐
2. Pleasant and easy to get along with?	☐	☐
3. Understanding and caring?	☐	☐
4. Flexible and open-minded?	☐	☐

Remember, Millennials as a group crave continual feedback and reinforcement. The previously listed managerial tactics that will help you meet requirements of the "boss factor" communication needs will also help to improve Millennial performance.

Recommendations to Meet Millennials' "Boss Factor" Communication Needs

After considering the previously listed expectations that Millennials have of their bosses, identify one or more of the following recommendations that can help you meet their needs.

____ 1. Don't wait for the annual performance review to provide feedback—give spot reviews as tasks and projects are completed.

____ 2. Be a fair-minded manager who dispenses advice, provides support, and then gives them space to do their jobs their own way.

____ 3. Provide open responses that are honest.

____ 4. Model the communication practices that you expect in others.

____ 5. Acknowledge your Millennials as both professionals and individuals. Recognize that they have lives outside of work.

____ 6. Acknowledge their ideas and encourage them to approach you with their thoughts.

What other recommendations would you make to meet the Millennials' communication needs?

____

____

____

____

The Coworker Factor and Millennial Communication Expectations

Robert Half International and Yahoo! Hot Jobs commissioned a national survey of more than a thousand adults, ages 21–28; the survey sampled an equal number of men and women. The findings were reported in *What Millennial Workers Want: How to Attract and Retain Gen Y Employees*. As the study reveals, while Internet technology has been fairly ubiquitous for this group, we are reminded not to assume that it is the Millennial's communication method of choice. Millennials are a highly social generation, accustomed to doing things as part of a group since their years in daycare and preschool. Two interesting findings from the study:

- Two-thirds of survey respondents selected in-person conversation with their coworkers as their preferred communication method.
- Only one in five would rather communicate by e-mail.

Communication Implications for Managers of Millennials

While effective management is both an art and a science, there are also research-based recommendations that can help meet Millennial communication needs. Here are four for your consideration.

1. Make sure your workplace is structured to encourage plenty of "face time," which Millennials enjoy.
2. Arrange workgroups in open, connected seating areas that facilitate face-to-face communication.
3. Create opportunities for employees to socialize during and after work (remember Part Three: Fun and Social Interaction).
4. The more Millennials feel connected to their co-workers, the more they are likely to be satisfied with their jobs and stay with your organization.

As we assess Millennial communication expectations, we find some interesting paradoxes. While Facebook may be a preferred way of social networking, face time emerges as a workplace communication preference. Just as Millennials demonstrate an impressive set of communication strengths, they also have their own set of skill deficits.

Millennial Communication Deficits

Here are a few examples of potential Millennial communication deficits that would profit from the manager and mentor's coaching.

- While "Generation Direct" can be an asset, as previously discussed, any strength can also be a weakness. Millennials could increase their communication effectiveness by being a little more cautious, politically aware, and sensitive in the way they respond.
- Millennials are excellent multitaskers. However, too much multitasking can undermine the effectiveness of interpersonal communication. Reading and responding to e-mail while talking to a colleague on the phone or face to face results in ineffective communication. In *The Trophy Kids Grow Up*, Ron Alsop writes, "Some critics even consider the Millennials' extreme multitasking a manifestation of an attention disorder and have labeled them the Ritalin Generation."
- Written communication in the form of memos, compelling documents, and letters appear to require remediation for Millennials, according to studies conducted by The Conference Board. Ron Alsop makes another compelling statement that "Employers are finding that this e-literate generation is barely literate in other forms of communication."

Strategies and Tactics

There is an infinite variety of strategies and tactics that a manager can use in establishing and sustaining effective communication. This section offers two sets of recommendations. First, a series of research-based recommendations by other authors and researchers is presented. Second, four best-of-class recommendations are presented by our Contributing Experts.

Research-based Strategies and Tactics for Effective Communication with Millennials

The title of this book should not imply that motivation is a separate competency that stands alone. Often, in one informal hallway meeting with a Millennial, a manager may find that he or she has to communicate, motivate, delegate, and perhaps resolve a conflict. However, by studying and mastering specific strategies and tactics of each critical managerial competency—especially communication—the manager can increase his or her effectiveness.

Research-Based Strategy One: Surefire Ways to Connect to Millennials

In virtually every study of Millennials, communication emerges as a dominant theme. Eric Chester, in *Employing Generation Why?,* stresses the importance of building an effective, ongoing communication relationship with Millennials. I have selected five relevant communication strategies for this part.

- **Keep positive today and be optimistic about tomorrow.**

  Both the United States and our broader global economy are rallying to respond to challenges that have not been experienced in decades. While it would be naïve to suggest that a manager present a distorted view of a severe workplace/workforce situation, he or she can certainly avoid appearing to be a prophet of doom. Rather, the manager has an opportunity to generate both physical and psychic energy by the words and actions presented each day. By presenting opportunities for Millennials to solve problems and to develop creative ideas, individuals and teams can generate psychic income.

- **Know the why; show the way.**

  While "Millennials" has come to be the most generally accepted term to describe what is now the twenty-something population, other authors and researchers have coined different labels. Eric Chester chooses to label the post–Generation Xers (born after 1980) as "Generation Why?" His reason, to quote him directly, is "Although they are better educated, more techno-savvy, and quicker to adapt than those who have come before them, they refuse to blindly conform to traditional standards and time-honored institutions. Instead, they boldly ask Why?"

With this explanation of "why," it is beneficial to respond to questions about the logic and reasoning of a manager's actions. In addition, the manager of Millennials can meet their employees' communication needs by anticipating and inviting questions.

- **Tell the truth.**

  This has been—and continues to be—a period of accelerated mergers, acquisitions, and business closures. Public- and private-sector leaders have been tried for fraud, misconduct, and a variety of other criminal acts. The Millennial generation, described by some as our hero generation, has great pride in their country, concern for the community, and respect for the environment. They value honesty and integrity.

  The more opportunities you seek to share timely, relevant information with Millennials, the more you can build trust in yourself and your organization.

- **Get to know them.**

  The bedrock principle of effective communication begins by understanding yourself. A corollary principle is "empathic communication." Stephen R. Covey wrote in *The Seven Habits of Effective People* that your effectiveness as a communicator is based not merely on communicating information, but also on an appreciation of how others will respond to the information. This principle takes on added value when you plan to delegate, motivate, and negotiate.

  How much do you know about your Millennials—not just their skill sets, but their interests, hobbies, and values? Do your management style and team structure provide opportunities for you to get to know employees and for them to get to know you and each other?

- **Be an example.**

  Historically, one career-related problem for knowledge workers has been the absence of leader/technologist role models. This is of increasing importance as Millennial knowledge workers identify the leader/mentor as a significant motivational factor. No longer is "Do as I say, not as I do" an acceptable response. Millennials thrive with leaders who model the behaviors they strive to achieve. In addition to seeking out a collegial relationship founded on respect, they crave that leader whom Warren Bennis describes as "the individual who will take you places that you would not have gone on your own."

  In addition, Millennials seek out leaders who can give and receive effective feedback—the heart of establishing and sustaining effective communication. Many technically educated knowledge workers are promoted into management positions because of their technical skills. If you happen to fall into this category, you may find the Interactive Behavioral Simulations® developed by Strategic Interactions, Inc., to be of value. Contributing Expert Jennell Evans of Strategic Interactions, Inc., presents this learning methodology later in this part.

Research-based Strategy Two

You may have attended supervisory or management development courses in the past. Perhaps you even taught a course to your colleagues. You probably have a fundamental appreciation of the following basic supervisory techniques:

1. Effective communication with others begins with understanding yourself.
2. Getting to know your colleagues and employees as unique individuals is invaluable.
3. Creating a comfortable and low-stress work environment reaps multiple rewards.
4. Communication is not a just-in-case situation, but an all-the-time need.
5. Developing others is significantly enhanced by effective delegation and mentoring.

And of course, the final test of your basic supervisory effectiveness is meeting the needs of both individuals and the organization. Authors Carolyn A. Martin, Ph.D., and Bruce Tulgan present a series of Communication Best Practices in their book *Managing the Generation Mix: From Collision to Collaboration*. These practices are relevant to establishing and sustaining effective communication not just with Millennials, but with your entire multigenerational workforce.

Martin and Tulgan make two important points:

1. As a manager, you can create the expectation that even in a hectic environment, communication on all projects, assignments, and important issues will be just in time, all the time.
2. Help teams create easy-to-use communication systems that facilitate good communication.

Communication Best Practices

Indicate which of the following practices you think have potential for use in your hectic environment. (This list of best practices may also provide you with an opportunity to assess and expand your communication strategies and tactics.)

____ 1. Seize informal timeouts (spontaneous moments to communicate)

____ 2. Establish formal timeouts (scheduled moments to communicate)

____ 3. Circulate everyone's to-do lists

____ 4. Publicize weekly accomplishments

____ 5. Create unique e-mail subject lines

____ 6. Encourage members to ask for help

____ 7. Create an expert's database

____ 8. Create a shared-notes system

____ 9. Hit the ground running with action-packed meetings

____ 10. Call an innovation summit quarterly or biannually

Practice What You Preach: Communication Strategies

The following list of best practices provides examples of how four organizations address the issue of establishing and sustaining effective communication with Millennials. Each strategy presents a different perspective that should enhance your resources.

Practice What You Preach

Sue McLeod, Senior Consultant
Hay Group

The younger generation like structure to understand the rules—what's expected to succeed now? What does it take to get ahead?

Clarify the rules

- Define the behaviors you need your employees to demonstrate.
- Define how behavioral expectations change with different levels or roles.
- Communicate these behaviors through the organization.
- Connect the behaviors to your organization's business, mission, and goals.

Younger employees pick up the difference between words and actions—and these disparities fuel their cynicism. They are also quick to call "foul" when they see that there are different rules for different people. These rules need to be woven into your "people processes"—evaluations, training and development, and recruitment—and they need to be applied consistently.

Walk the talk

- Include information about your expectations in the recruiting process.
- Use interview techniques that screen job candidates' behaviors as well as their skills and experience.
- Ensure that managers communicate expectations and give frequent feedback to reinforce the desired behaviors.
- Incorporate behavioral expectations into formal performance reviews.
- Provide opportunities for employees to develop and demonstrate new behaviors needed for advancement, through coaching, mentoring, training, and new work assignments.
- Hold everyone accountable for demonstrating important behaviors.

Interactive Behavioral Simulations®

Jennell Evans, President and CEO
Strategic Interactions, Inc.

Millennials want consistent feedback on "how they are doing," "how they can improve," and "how they can move up" more frequently than any other generation. Their desire for sustained communication can create challenges with co-workers and managers less inclined to take time to give feedback or share information in general. The reality is that Millennials expect their manager to take the time to give feedback, or they may seek a different employer who understands how important it is to provide this kind of communication.

A lot of workplace research confirms that the primary reason most people leave their jobs is that they do not have a good relationship with their managers. Because excellent communication is key to good relationships, it is important that organizations give people the tools and resources (i.e., communication skills training) to successfully manage relationships in the workplace.

One of the fundamental responsibilities of a manager is to give feedback to those he or she supervises. At Strategic Interactions, we worked with an organization that wanted to provide feedback skills training to managers, most of whom supervised younger workers. The client's data from exit interviews confirmed that the organization was losing young talent because managers did not give them feedback, or when they did, it was not specific or timely.

Most people avoid giving feedback because they do not know how to do it, especially if they know the person needs to be doing something better. People need to learn *how* to give feedback through real-life experiences, so they understand their own responses in feedback situations, as well as understanding what the person receiving the feedback may be experiencing.

To help this client stop the loss of young talent, we designed a simulation-based half-day workshop to demonstrate the behavioral aspects of giving feedback, and we included information about generational diversity. This highly experiential workshop allowed the managers (engineers) to practice giving feedback without any risk of "saying things the wrong way" and potentially damaging the relationship. In essence, we created a "learning lab," where managers could observe how to give feedback and try out different strategies within their own comfort zone. One specific simulation involved a Boomer giving feedback to a Millennial. The simulation allowed the Boomer to better understand the Millennial's perspective regarding feedback, as well as learn skills in giving feedback that the Millennial could understand and make a plan to improve.

The client validated through internal measures that the managers who attended the training had significantly higher retention rates than managers who had not attended the training.

Effective Recruiting, On-boarding, and Assimilation Examples

Marcia Riley, Vice President, Talent Management and Human Resources
ESI International

When I received a job offer from John Elsey, President and CEO of ESI International, I hesitated because of the long commute from Silver Spring to Arlington each day. He actually did some research for me. He got in his car and drove several routes and e-mailed me with the fastest route. It was an exceptional and thoughtful "best practice" that took my breath away. I accepted the position!

While I was serving at Inova Health System as their very first Chief Learning Officer, we hired two individuals who had not yet met and who would be working very closely together. I suggested that they meet for breakfast or lunch at the company's expense before they started, so that on day one they would have a friend and begin working as a team. Both stayed with Inova for many years and were key contributors during their tenure at the organization. To this day, I get calls from them telling me how much that meeting mattered to their on-boarding at Inova. They always remembered how special that was, and they were an outstanding team for many years.

When we hire new employees at ESI, we check in with them at 45 days. Many organizations check in with managers to see how their new employees are doing. At ESI, we believe that work is about trust and open communication. As the vice president of Talent Management and Human Resources, I sit down with every new employee to make sure that we are living up to our promises as their new employer. We do not have an issue with turnover because we keep in touch with our employees and they know that their satisfaction with our organization is important to us.

Member Partnership Management Framework (MPMF)

Shaara Roman, Director of Human Resources
CGI Federal

To help managers communicate better, CGI's ISO-9001 certified Member Partnership Management Framework (MPMF) establishes communication channels and processes between management and members that the management team of each business unit is accountable for following. In fact, their compensation is tied to their MPMF compliance.

Through a prescribed set of activities, including new employee orientation and integration, performance and career management, and ongoing one-on-one and team meetings, we build strong and long-term relationships with our members. The MPMF provides for ongoing measurement and improvement processes where members, as owners, are inspired to grow the company and are empowered to build a challenging and rewarding career.

MANAGER APPLICATION EXERCISE

Based on your review of the previous Contributing Expert strategies, specify those concepts most relevant to your establishing and sustaining effective communication with your Millennials.

1. ______________________________
2. ______________________________
3. ______________________________
4. ______________________________
5. ______________________________

Collaboration Technologies

Each new Millennial study, publication, and performance improvement program provides a different perspective on how to motivate the Millennial knowledge worker and improve performance. The most recent of these studies and books clearly address the importance of understanding these new "digital natives" and "technophiles." The following quote from Ron Alsop's book *The Trophy Kids Grow Up* captures the unique, critically important, and dominant Millennial characteristic.

> ***"Millennials are so tied to technology tools that they may be 10 feet away from you but still send a text message or e-mail rather than simply call out to you. Millennials have even been known to quit their jobs by e-mail. Yet as many impatient Millennials might say, e-mail is sooo dead. It's the new snail mail. Millennials expect rapid-fire feedback and get bored in a New York minute. No, make that a nanosecond… Now, texting on cell phones, instant messaging, and sending messages on social networking sites have become their preferred modes of communication."***
>
> **–Ron Alsop**

While this quote may capture a unique behavioral communication characteristic of Millennials, Rob Salkowitz takes this a step further. His book *Generation Blend: Managing Across the Technology Age Gap* addresses a critical point. "The arrival of the Millennials and the impact of Web 2.0 technology in the enterprise create unprecedented complexity for employers and workers in the 2010s and beyond." In Salkowitz's discussion of Millennials in the workforce, he demonstrates the interplay of Millennial characteristics, priorities, work styles, and of course, technology.

Technology Implications of Millennial Characteristics, Priorities, and Work Styles

Millennials see technology as a tool to provide:

- Social networks and contact management tools
- Real-time communication
- Open communication and information channels
- Expertise location systems
- Two-way channels of internal communication
- Blogs and other channels for personal expression
- Remote access and mobility, and access to personal networks at work
- Communication and collaboration systems, portals, workspaces, or teamware
- User environments that allow for shifting context

As Rob Salkowitz points out, "the generational personality of Millennials and their close relationship with technology has several implications for their future as participants in the workforce." However, many organizations still function with traditional channels of communication. These traditional channels do not meet the Millennials' need to be heard on the job and to receive frequent and useful feedback. The following statement is a wake-up call for all managers and human resources professionals: "Since they [Millennials] tend to be tribal and socially networked, they want sociable workplaces; they want to connect with others (including mentors)."

Further Discussion

Shira Harrington, Director, Professional Search *Positions Inc.*

The author, in describing why communication strategies often fail, makes a profound point when he says, "What is needed is ongoing and varied follow-up to sustain and support the process." He goes on to note that the second reason communication fails is that it "is not thought of as a shared responsibility between two individuals, most often a manager and an employee."

Looking beyond generational diversity for a moment, we could see truly effective communication as the essence of harmony in the workplace (and in the world, for that matter). When we focus on two-way communication—i.e., when both parties ask thought-provoking, non-judgmental questions, receive constructive feedback, and share suggestions aimed at mutual benefit—productivity naturally increases because the goal is success, not control over an individual.

Even discussing this concept is a paradigm shift from the business practices of the Veteran generation, who used a command-and-control style of supervision to cajole—or even force—performance out of their direct reports. Now that Baby Boomers have instituted a more collaborative style of performance management, the challenge is to arrive at a level of communication that moves beyond top-down management and includes Millennials (and all generations) as partners in corporate achievement.

While the topic of business communication is not a new one, using generational diversity as a "back door" training technique with managers could be a novel approach, such as that instituted by Strategic Interactions, Inc., in its simulated-feedback learning labs. We know that when placed in positions of leadership, most people either shy away from giving feedback or feel the need to assert their authority. Since neither tactic will work effectively with Millennials, now is the time to focus on unique strategies that will allow managers to safely explore ways to bring out the best performance in their young partners.

Thinking longer term, future research should address the coaching of Millennials who have already entered into management positions. Many of these ambitious protégés have been creating a unique challenge for their direct reports (who could be of any generation) due to their tendency to collaborate endlessly without making authoritative decisions. Compounded by their general avoidance of conflict, this generation has an even greater need for effective communications training.

Whether 75 years old or 25 years old, all employees could use extra learning support in the area of communication. We would do well to put into practice the famous axiom, "Seek first to understand before seeking to be understood."

Summary

Part Five's objectives focused on four key points. First, a review of a "Portrait of a Millennial" reinforced the importance of establishing and sustaining effective communication. Second, establishing and sustaining effective communication was presented as a shared responsibility of manager and Millennial. Third, strategies and tactics that managers can use to establish and sustain effective communication were emphasized. Fourth, collaboration technologies were described as promising new information tools for enterprises and critically important communication tools for Millennials.

P A R T 6

The Three R's: Recognition, Reward, and Respect

> ***"Meet Generation Y, the most high-maintenance workforce in the history of the world. It is also a generation that we desperately need to be creative, productive, and efficient in these challenging times."***
>
> **–Bruce Tulgan,** *Not Everyone Gets a Trophy*

In this part:

- Getting Started
- Generational Factors
- Recognition for the Millennial Knowledge Worker
- Applying Reward Strategies
- The Third R: Respect

Getting Started

As with previous parts of this book, this part is driven by our survey of Millennial motivational factors. Responses that are relevant to this part include “recognition,” “treatment as colleagues,” “interest in employees,” “respect,” “personal goals,” “generous time off, “rewards,” “promoted quickly,” and “comprehensive benefits.” After the data were analyzed, similar descriptors of motivational factors were combined, and recognition, reward, and respect emerged as compatible motivational factors.

Further research and Contributing Experts’ recommendations result in this part’s focus on the following four objectives:

- Identify those unique generational factors that influence the importance of recognition, reward, and respect as Millennial motivators.
- Appreciate the importance of appropriate recognition for the Millennial knowledge worker.
- Establish an organizational and managerial climate to apply reward strategies.
- Develop a mutually beneficial climate in support of respect.

Generational Factors

There is substantial research to support the statement that unique generational factors have influenced the importance of recognition, reward, and respect as Millennial motivators. Since William Strauss and Neil Howe introduced the concept of generational personalities with their now classic 1991 book, *Generations: The History of America's Future, 1584-2069,* a well-documented body of literature has suggested that methods of generational analysis can be applied to organizations as a system to attract, recruit, develop, manage, motivate, and retain all generational cohorts.

A casual review of the events and factors that have shaped the behaviors and values of the Millennials demonstrates why they value recognition, reward, and respect.

DID YOU KNOW?

The social context for those growing up as the Millennial generation (born between 1982 and 2003) is characterized by a number of factors.

Yes	No	Did you know that...
☐	☐	1. During this period there was a shift back to a child-centered social context.
☐	☐	2. This time period represented the lowest child-parent ratio in American history. Terms like "soccer mom" and "Baby on Board" emerged.
☐	☐	3. Children were cherished, nurtured, and encouraged to excel at school, immerse themselves in a broad range of extracurricular activities, and even prepare for college while in elementary school.
☐	☐	4. With this achievement-driven, parent-nurtured background—"you are special," "you can be whatever you want to be"—Millennials emerged as a career-oriented generation.
☐	☐	5. They graduated from college and expected to be catered to and to receive constant recognition and feedback.

Neil Howe and William Strauss wrote in their 1991 book, *Millennials Rising*:

> ***"They're the most watched over generation in memory. Each year, adults subject the typical kid's day to ever more structure and supervision, making it a nonstop round of parents, relatives, teachers, coaches, baby-sitters, counselors, chaperones, minivans, surveillance cams, and curfews."***

It is apparent why recognition, reward, and respect are important to Millennials. It is not surprising that titles such as *The Trophy Kids Grow Up: How the Millennial Generation Is Shaking Up the Workplace* are appearing. A chapter in Bruce Tulgun's new book, *Not Everyone Gets a Trophy,* suggests that leaders and human resources professionals must practice "*in loco parentis* management."

Recognition for the Millennial Knowledge Worker

In the dictionary, "recognize" is defined as "to acknowledge or to take notice of in some definite way." Recognition is also part of a continuous retention system described, in *Workforce Crisis*, as "Attentive management, where the direct manager not only appreciates employees' points of view [and contributions], but also attends to the employee's needs and progress and explicitly encourages—and is accountable for—retention." Taking the definition a step further, recognition, rewards, and respect are part of a broader motivational and retention strategy that links the human resources workforce plan to tangible business outcomes. It is all part of a comprehensive strategy that helps management avoid excessive costs, optimize productivity, and beat the competition to market.

While the early part of this chapter discusses the Three R's—recognition, reward, and respect—separately, they are actually concurrent motivational factors. Perhaps another way to view these components is as an equation:

Recognition + Rewards + Respect = Repeated High Performance

Strategies to Meet the Recognition Needs of Millennial Knowledge Workers

The earlier description of Millennials suggests that they expect their managers to be similar to their parents, teachers, and coaches. Millennials have been described as "crying out to management" to recognize and praise them. They are drawn to organizations and managers that offer frequent recognition. They are quick to leave those that don't give it. The positive aspect of this need for recognition is that when they receive it in a timely and authentic manner, they have a proven track record of exceeding normal expectations.

The Four P's of "Wise Recognition and Rewards"

Earlier discussion suggests that opportunities to meet the Millennials' needs for recognition, rewards, and respect often occur concurrently. From this perspective, Eric Chester, in his book *Employing Generation Why? Understanding, Managing and Motivating Your New Workforce*, presents four criteria for "wise recognition and rewards."

1. **Personal**

    ▷ The perceived value of recognition or a reward escalates when it is individualized.

    ▷ Look for formal and informal opportunities to get to know what employees like to do in their personal time away from work.

    ▷ Demonstrate this knowledge when you customize the recognition or rewards you give.

2. **Proportionate**

    ▷ A reward or recognition should match the level of performance being recognized.

    ▷ Plan your recognition and reward program to make certain that it includes various levels of achievement.

    ▷ Avoid heaping praise on minor task assignments that are a routine part of the job.

3. **Punctual**

    Millennials live in the moment. As a manager or human resources professional, you know that the closer to the accomplishment that recognition or a reward is given, the more effective it is. With this in mind, you are encouraged to:

    ▷ Develop a recognition and reward inventory that is ready to be used at the appropriate time (gift cards, tickets to sporting events, time off, etc.).

    ▷ Prepare to give unscheduled spot awards to enhance your unit's motivational climate.

    ▷ Deliver the recognition or reward today, rather than promise it for tomorrow.

4. **Public**

    "Praise in public, censure in private" is a Supervision 202 principle. Yet often it is not practiced to the degree it should be. Here are three recommendations.

    ▷ Present recognition and rewards in the presence of the employee's peers. This will multiply the value exponentially.

    ▷ Consider sharing the news of recognition or rewards in an e-mail message or on a website.

    ▷ Take advantage of coffee breaks, luncheons, or dinners to "seize the moment" to announce an unanticipated act of recognition or reward.

The Four P's of Wise Recognition and Rewards are sound management practices that are especially relevant to meeting the motivational needs of the Millennial knowledge worker, who thrives on spontaneity, positive feedback, and social work environments.

APPLICATION EXERCISE: THE FOUR P'S OF RECOGNITION AND REWARDS

Select one tactic from each of the Four P's of Recognition and Rewards that you will apply to improve your Millennial recognition and reward strategies. Record your tactics in the action plan below.

1. Personal: ______________________________

2. Proportionate: ______________________________

3. Punctual: ______________________________

4. Public: ______________________________

Make note of another recognition and reward tactic from your own experiences that is especially relevant to the Millennials.

____

Contributing Experts: Two Perspectives

The contents of this book have been significantly shaped by the expertise, interest, and guidance of Contributing Experts. At this point in the part, two Contributing Experts are featured. The first, Shaara Roman, provides a unique description of a multilevel corporate recognition program. The second, Rick Humphress, presents best-of-class practices and a recognition checklist. He then introduces a research-based recognition model that serves as a framework for application and further discussion.

Each organization has an unlimited opportunity to initiate a comprehensive recognition program. Often a program's strategies and tactics were initiated at different times in response to different needs in terms of corporate communication, organizational development, and motivation. In addition, a recognition program may respond to local, regional, and national needs. The examples presented by Shaara Roman showcase such a model.

A Multilevel Corporate Recognition Program

Shaara Roman, Director, Human Resources
CGI Federal

CGI Federal provides a number of recognition and reward programs for our members.

- **The Builders Award program** — Members who have contributed significantly to the growth of our company are recognized via our annual Builders Award program. They are invited to an awards ceremony held during our annual Vice Presidents Conference and are presented with a commemorative plaque by our founder, Serge Godin, and our CEO, Michael E. Roach. A framed photograph of each honoree is also displayed at a local office of his or her choice, as well as in our corporate headquarters in Montreal. Approximately ten people are chosen for this prestigious award each year.
- **The Excellence in Innovation Awards program** — This annual awards program recognizes members who have developed tools, frameworks, methodologies, or processes that benefit the company or our clients in some major way. Significant cash prizes are awarded, including a $10,000 prize for the winning individual submission, and a $25,000 prize for the winning team submission (split among team members). The winners, the number of which varies from year to year, are presented with an engraved award and cash prizes by senior management during our Member Annual Tour.

- **The Service Recognition program** — Through this program, CGI recognizes important milestones in a member's career at CGI, including his or her third, fifth, tenth, fifteenth, twentieth, twenty-fifth, and thirtieth anniversaries. Ceremonies are held during the regular team meetings within each business unit so that members can be recognized by their peers. Members are also recognized during our Member Annual Tour and in company publications. The program also provides a choice of gift, the value of which varies according to the number of years of service. In addition, members completing 25 years of service are awarded a one-time bonus of five extra vacation days.
- **Above & Beyond, and the CGI Showcase** — Stories of members who have excelled in their work are featured regularly in the Above & Beyond and CGI Showcase sections of our global member newsletter, as well as in a news section on our enterprise portal. Members are invited on an ongoing basis to submit stories.
- **The CGI Federal Recognition program** — The Stars program gives members an opportunity to nominate their colleagues for recognition. Those chosen for recognition receive a commemorative gift and a gift card. They also receive coverage in local publications and are eligible for an annual award.
- **The Member Partnership Management Framework** — In addition to our formal recognition programs, CGI's ISO-9001 certified Member Partnership Management Framework encourages informal recognition of members during quarterly "All Hands" team meetings.

Best-of-Class Practices, a Checklist, and a Model

Rick Humphress, Public Sector, Human Capital Management
Oracle Corporation

A preliminary review of Contributing Experts' Motivational Indicators outlines three interrelated and significant Millennial Motivational Factors. A direct quote of several statements captures the importance of this part. First, Millennials expect appreciation and recognition for their efforts and ideas. Their expectation is that this recognition is frequent and often presented in front of their peers. One form of recognition that is especially meaningful is recognition from senior management and increased visibility in the organization.

Along with the importance of recognition is the importance of respect. As one Millennial stated, "Ask me for my input and listen to my ideas." Respect for ideas is a critical motivator. The recognition and respect equation is further reinforced by a variety of diverse and timely rewards. As one important example, Millennials view increased responsibility as a reward. They clearly and aggressively seek greater responsibility as a reward for accomplishment. And the range of rewards varies with the individuals. In addition to salary, they seek a diverse menu of rewards that can be tailored to their individual motivational profile. A quick promotion and change of job title or the opportunity for accelerated learning may be examples of "one size does not fit all."

Perhaps one of the greatest Millennial motivational challenges is reconciling the business needs of the organization and the motivational preferences of Millennials. The desire to be treated as respected colleagues—despite age, position title, and responsibility—is a key driver of the Millennial motivators of recognition, respect, and rewards.

Best-in-Class Practices

Recognition is a form of appreciation that gives people a positive attitude about their ability to contribute to a team or organization. Research in industrial psychology shows that by setting, achieving, and recognizing goals and goal achievement, organizations will be more successful. The following represents a set of best-in-class practices and considerations that an organization can use to guide the implementation of a recognition program to benefit all employees regardless of their sociological grouping (Traditionalists, Baby Boomers, Gen Xers, or Millennials).

- **First, do no harm.** Organizations should examine their practices and methods of delivering recognition and should stop de-motivating activities.
- **Everyone can be praised.** Recognition should be awarded on a straight-line basis: set criteria and reward everyone who meets them. Do not set up a win-lose culture by recognizing only the top performance.
- **Recognition must be motivational.** It should be fair, consistent, timely, specific, and intermittent. Otherwise, it may become an expected entitlement and lose its motivational qualities.
- **Tailor recognition.** Based upon age, employees belong to broad sociological groups associated with specific characteristics. However, each of these employees also has an individual personality, and recognition should be tailored to the needs of the individual for it to be truly motivational.

- **Differentiate incentive programs from recognition programs.** Incentive programs publicly identify in advance precise behaviors rewarded with specific rewards. Recognition programs reward specific desirable behaviors after the fact.
- **Public recognition is not always best.** Since good performance is an exceptional event (a unique person performing a certain behavior at a specific time), it should be recognized in a private, one-on-one setting. One notable exception is group recognition.
- **Encourage positive gossip.** When a peer employee or a manager in another division compliments superior performance, use this as the basis to recognize an employee. It will be perceived as more genuine and it will promote social cohesion because an employee cannot help but feel closer to a person who genuinely praises him or her.
- **Train employees how to give recognition.** Keep the praise simple, and any rewards, symbolic. Sandwiching corrective feedback between two slices of recognition can work very well because it softens the blow. Many Millennials are very sensitive to any corrective feedback, so managers need to be delicate in how they deliver it.
- **Train employees how to receive recognition.** Employees need to engage in behaviors that encourage managers to give recognition, including avoiding disclaimer statements, showing sincere appreciation, valuing the recognition, and giving reciprocal recognition for the praise.

Checklist

To implement a best-in-class recognition program:

- ❑ Examine existing recognition practices and eliminate those that do not produce any motivational benefits or are de-motivating.
- ❑ Clearly articulate the organizational differences between an incentive program (known rewards, known time frame) and recognition (unknown rewards, unknown time frame).
- ❑ Determine criteria or standards of behavior worthy of recognition.
- ❑ Determine what kind of recognition would uniquely motivate each employee.
- ❑ Train recognition givers and receivers on optimal methods to give and receive rewards.
- ❑ Track recognition and performance appraisals to determine the impact of recognition on job performance.

Models

Organizations give recognition to motivate employees and to encourage productive work behaviors. Recognition is a primary positive reinforcement because it strengthens an existing behavior. The question arises of what pattern of recognition delivers the highest motivation, as measured by the number of positive work behaviors. Research shows that the best recognition would occur not after every positive instance, but rather after a variable number of positive instances. A variable ratio schedule of VR-10, for instance, means that on average, recognition follows every tenth instance of good work behavior. Variable recognition keeps the employee guessing when the next payoff of praise will occur. This schedule of recognition generates the highest rate of response of any alternative.

	Ratio	Interval
Variable	**VR:** The number of positive work behaviors required before recognition occurs varies from one period to the next. VR-10 indicates that recognition is given, on average, after every tenth positive work behavior.	**VI:** After a variable period of time (interval), the first positive work behavior is recognized. VI-10 indicates that recognition is given immediately after an average of ten units of time have passed.
Fixed	**FR:** The number of positive work behaviors required before recognition occurs is a fixed number. FR-10 indicates that recognition is given after every tenth positive work behavior.	**FI:** After a fixed time interval, the first positive work behavior is recognized. FI-10 indicates that recognition is given immediately after ten units of time have passed.

Additional Recognition Strategies

A broad variety of recognition strategies are available to meet the motivational needs of Millennials. In addition to those previously presented, the following examples are provided. As Ken Blanchard, known for his situational leadership methodology, suggests, "One size does not fit all." He once said that "What motivates people is what motivates people." This concept is especially important in selecting the appropriate recognition strategy for your Millennials, while recognizing that within their generational band, there are opportunities to customize and tailor strategies and tactics to meet individual needs. With this concept in mind, the following recognition strategies are presented. Select those that are most appropriate for the individual Millennial whom you have identified to recognize.

MILLENNIAL RECOGNITION STRATEGIES

Identify a specific recognition strategy that would be most appropriate for an individual member of your team.

____ 1. **Recognize the whole person.** As Part One: Flexibility and Work/Life Balance stressed, Millennials place considerable importance on a balanced life, in which work is only one component of their "get a life" portfolio. Work is a means to an end; it is not an end in itself. One way to recognize this healthy priority is to gain a deeper and more detailed understanding of your individual Millennials. A sincere and appropriate interest in an employee's personal life can create a bond and trust, which benefit both individual and organization.

____ 2. **Promote and reinforce excellence.** Many Millennials work in rapidly changing, high-productivity, task-driven environments. Individuals who demonstrate skill in multitasking often work on concurrent projects with multiple formal and informal reporting lines. In this environment, managers may miss—and underestimate—the value of promoting and reinforcing excellence on a continuous basis. This form of recognition, "psychic income," can range from a formal, scheduled event to more informal and spontaneous recognition. This could be done through e-mail, a website, a meeting announcement, gift certificates, or an electronic scorecard that reinforces organizational values.

____ 3. **Recognize and address Millennial generational priorities.** Author Rob Salkowitz discusses this concept as it relates to generational technology implications. However, the concept also applies to other workplace and Millennial cultural implications. The following two examples are presented as potential Millennial generational recognition motivators.

Example 1: Millennials value gaining approval and recognition. This requires providing more hands-on management with direct communication and feedback.

Example 2: Millennials value making a difference. This requires providing more opportunities for participation in shaping policies.

Applying Reward Strategies

Motivating Millennial knowledge workers through the use of recognition, reward, and respect strategies is not a tedious managerial task. In *Motivating the "What's In It For Me?" Workforce,* Cam Marston makes this very point in stating that "One way to create the behavior you're looking for is to find ways to recognize and reward the desired behaviors in your workforce and then to celebrate them."

The importance of rewards is not new. Virtually every basic management or organizational behavior book presents the concept of rewards. It is, as defined in *Understanding People: Models and Concepts*, "the means and methods a manager uses for rewarding (or punishing) employees for their behavior, including strategies he/she uses, if any, for motivating them and the atmosphere he/she establishes, which lead employees to anticipate being rewarded or punished for certain kinds of behavior." While the importance of rewards has not changed, what has changed is the type of reward each of the four generations identifies as being of unique importance to them.

Portrait of Millennials: A Behavioral Review

A review of select Millennial behavioral characteristics highlights the relevance and importance of recognition and reward strategies.

- Millennials tend to be very career oriented and expect rapid advancement and perks.
- Millennials appreciate feedback, having been graded, evaluated, and ranked throughout their lives.
- They want frequent communication from their boss.
- They are motivated to contribute beyond what is expected of their formal position.
- They believe that the better the performance, the better their opportunity for advancement.
- Managers need to get a sense of how Millennials like to be praised—in public, in team meetings, or one-on-one in the office.
- They want to take charge. They believe they deserve a trophy, whether they win or lose.
- They want to add value through their ideas, their analyses, and their judgment.
- They are independent, techno-savvy, entrepreneurial hard workers who thrive on flexibility.

What Do Millennial Knowledge Workers Want from their Jobs?

We are focusing on Millennials who are also knowledge workers. I have daily contact with this group, as I write this book from the Greater Washington D.C. area, where Millennial knowledge workers are sought after despite a national economic downturn. I agree wholeheartedly with the research-based Millennial expectations that follow.

Millennial Expectations

Among the nine expectations presented in "What Do Young Workers Expect from Work?" and "What Matters to Young Workers?" in *Workforce Crisis* are the following relevant Millennial motivational factors of rewards, recognition, and respect. One definition of motivation is meeting the individual's desires, wants, and needs.

- "Individual responsibility, freedom to make decisions"
- "Opportunities to learn and grow"
- "Team-based work, collaborative decision making"
- "Lots of feedback, frequent and constructive reviews"
- "Work that is personally stimulating and enjoyable"
- "Work that is worthwhile to society"

Millennial Knowledge Workers and Rewards

As there is a growing body of literature about Millennials, there is a corresponding body of literature about knowledge workers. With these resources available, there is a rich library of reward strategies and tactics to employ. Opportunities exist to customize motivational strategies to meet the needs of each Millennial. The following discussion of rewards combines recommendations of a noted author and Contributing Experts.

An Author/Researcher's Perspective

Frances Horibe, writing in *Managing Knowledge Workers,* raises several questions that the reader/practitioner needs to address. She discusses how organizational rewards contribute to employee satisfaction and retention. She also delineates three types of rewards—money, personal awards, and awards programs—as they relate to the motivational needs of knowledge workers. Strategies and tactics have been selected from her book to create the following organizational inventory.

How Do You Reward Knowledge Workers: An Organizational Inventory

Indicate which of the following reward tactics you currently use or should use.

Money: This includes bonuses, incentive programs, profit sharing, stock options, and salary.

____ 1. Competing on price. Do you pay competitive salaries? Does it enable you to increase the service you provide in support of existing production and innovations?

____ 2. Diminishing returns. Does money, in the form of increased salaries, maintain its motivational value? Or are there other factors equally or more critical to retaining your Millennial knowledge workers?

____ 3. Is money the best way to recruit and maintain your intellectual capital?

____ 4. Be-all and end-all. Money isn't the driver many people think it is. Your competitive edge is considering other rewards to recruit, reward, and retain Millennial knowledge workers.

Personal: Frances Horibe introduces praise as a motivational strategy relevant to knowledge workers, and provides examples of praise. Here are six types for your consideration.

____ 1. Praise something the employee cares about.

____ 2. Praise patterns as well as extraordinary efforts.

____ 3. Praise the characteristic or trait, not just the activity.

____ 4. Praise only what you believe is important.

____ 5. Separate praise and opportunities for improvement.

____ 6. Tell the person how you really feel about their work.

CONTINUED

CONTINUED

Award Programs: Award programs go beyond personal recognition given as a reward and become a more formal part of the organizational culture. However, they are often a collection of activities that individually and collectively lose their potential. As Horibe writes, "Unless formal recognition programs help people stand a little taller and prouder, they have no value."

There are three ways to strengthen your organization's award program for knowledge workers. They are:

____ 1. Decide what you want from the award program.

____ 2. Maximize your success in designing award programs for knowledge workers that are clearly valued.

____ 3. Appreciate that creating new knowledge is an important motivator for knowledge workers. Their need for external awards is not as great as for other types of workers.

Critical Factors for Reward Program Success

Sue McLeod, Senior Consultant
Hay Group

Our research shows that the most successful reward programs work because they have been well implemented, rather than neatly designed. This implementation requires a strong partnership between Human Resources and line managers. We've identified six key rules that organizations should follow when putting their reward programs in action:

1. Don't leave the job of implementing reward programs solely to HR.
2. Use line managers to communicate the intent and rationale of the reward program to employees.
3. Ensure that HR makes the goals of the reward program clear and easy to understand.
4. Communicate the total value of the organization's reward program by using individualized total reward statements.
5. Encourage line managers to make use of the entire palette of your rewards, including intangible rewards, to motivate employees.
6. Make sure that HR provides line managers with the necessary tools and backup to help them effectively communicate the benefits of the program to employees.

A strategy or tactic, no matter how well designed, is only as effective as its implementation. And in the previous case, it requires a collaborative effort between the line manager and the human resources professional—the target audiences for this book.

Millennial Reward Assumptions: A Shared Responsibility

Many of our reader/practitioners are familiar with the concept of employee contracts. In many cases, the concept is limited to a letter of employment, much like a prenuptial agreement, that spells out the terms of employment and includes the familiar clause stating that both employer and employee can part ways at any time without an explanation. However, in more sophisticated organizational cultures, and under the leadership of the human resources professional and senior management, the "social" and "psychological" contracts are discussed and initiated that enable the employee to feel more part of the organization and its respective culture.

The Millennial Reward Contract

It has become quite apparent, based on numerous research studies, books, and the work of consultants, that Millennials have a set of clearly defined reward expectations. And while there is no proven formula that works in all organizations or for all professionals, in general the following three Millennial reward assumptions deserve consideration.

THREE ASSUMPTIONS ABOUT REWARDS FOR MILLENNIAL KNOWLEDGE WORKERS

Indicate how well you and your organization effectively meet the following three assumptions.

❑ 1. **The Millennials' high expectations**

For a variety of reasons discussed in previous parts of this book, one of the most noticeable characteristics of Millennials is a strong sense of entitlement. This "What's In It for Me?" generation begins employment with each new job with extremely high expectations. Virtually every book or study on the topic describes their desire for fast promotions and frequent performance feedback, while prioritizing their need for work/life balance and participation in community service. In fact, the traditional concept of work/life balance has taken on an expanded meaning for Millennials. They now think in terms of "work-life integration." More specifically, they view work and life as a blend. Personal life comes into work, and work comes into personal life. This is a new reality for the Millennial.

CONTINUED

CONTINUED

- [ ] 2. **The manager's role in outlining goals and rewards**

    The concept of introducing a performance management model is not new or novel. Basic Supervision and Introduction to Management courses include a model that begins by stressing step one as setting goals and communicating expectations. However, this concept is even more important for Millennials. Lisa Orrell, in *Millennials Incorporated,* states, "Clearly outline goals and rewards for everything. Be very clear on what you want done and what they will get when it's done."

- [ ] 3. **Rewarding work behavior—the manager's roles**

    Abraham Maslow wrote extensively about motivation. One observation he made was that most employees want to do a good job and like to be told when they have done a good job. Unfortunately, many managers do not provide this positive feedback often enough. Rewarding good performance and providing consistent positive feedback takes on critical importance to a generation used to instant feedback and gratification from parents, teachers, coaches, and community.

Application Exercise

After reviewing the three previous assumptions, I can better meet the reward motivational needs of Millennial knowledge workers by:

___

___

___

___

Three Reward Strategies Beyond Money

Salary cannot be dismissed as a critically important recruiting and retention tool for Millennial knowledge workers. In a survey commissioned by Robert Half International and Yahoo! HotJobs, with results published in *What Millennial Workers Want: How to Attract and Retain Gen Y Employees*, employees ranked salary a 9.5 in importance on a 1-to-10 scale, with 10 being the most important. However, most experienced managers and HR professionals also know that it is one of the most short-lived motivators unless a balanced portfolio of reward strategies exists. In fact, many of us already know that some of the important Millennial reward strategies may cost the least and benefit Millennials and the organization the most. Here are two critically important reward strategies and several examples for each category for your consideration.

Make Increased Responsibility a Reward

Every behavior can be viewed as both a strength and a weakness. For example, Millennials have high expectations for fast promotions and frequent feedback. They have also been described as multitaskers with an insatiable appetite for increased responsibility. The opportunity to maximize this behavioral trait is further reinforced by an examination of terms appearing in the Motivational Factors Survey that shaped this book. Those behavior preferences included:

Career advancement	Fast-cycle work environment
Challenging work	Accomplishment
Passion for work	Trail blazing
Immediacy	Quick promotions
Adaptability	Empowerment
Accomplishment	Treatment as colleagues

As Lisa Orrell suggests in *Millennials Incorporated,* "New challenges and constant stimulation keep them motivated. This doesn't mean constantly having to promote them! Find ways to challenge them within their current positions until they deserve to be promoted."

Learning as a Reward

An organization's building intellectual capital and managing knowledge workers implies opportunities for continuous learning where there is a tendency to consider learning itself as a reward. In fact, an organization's ability to manage knowledge and meet Millennials' learning needs has become a predominant characteristic to be considered. Michael J. Marquardt, author of *Building Learning Organizations,* reinforces this point in stating that "To succeed in the fast-changing globally competitive business environment of today, an organization must have the capacity to continually learn from its experiences … and translate that knowledge into improved performance." Several of his strategies use learning to motivate Millennial knowledge workers. The following exercise is based on material in Marquardt's book, *Building Learning Organizations*.

MOTIVATING MILLENNIAL KNOWLEDGE WORKERS: A STRATEGIES CHECKLIST

Indicate which of the following strategies you currently employ and which strategies you might employ in the future.

Currently Use	Should Use	
❑	❑	Recognize and reward learning
❑	❑	Build learning into all operations and activities
❑	❑	Intertwine and align organizational learning with business and personal success
❑	❑	Set aside time for learning
❑	❑	Measure and broadcast the impact and benefits of learning
❑	❑	Maximize learning on the job

As a result of providing increased responsibility and learning as rewards, I will apply the following strategy:

____

____

____

Rewarding Performance

While rewarding performance is a recommended and accepted practice in managing and supervising others, the generational literature suggests that rewarding the "most coddled generation in history" requires special attention. Contributing Expert Rick Humphress has previously suggested that treating each generation with "generalized motivational strategies" may overlook the individual differences that often exist within the same generation.

Contributing Expert Sue McLeod presents Hay Group's research-based recommendation of rewarding Millennial performance. She writes:

The younger generation may be used to "everyone gets a trophy," but you know that won't help your organization succeed. Treating everyone the same can demoralize the best and create a sense of entitlement for the rest.

On the other hand, Millennials are used to being graded, getting feedback, and knowing where they stand against standards of performance. At the same time, they have a strong desire to get ahead and want support and encouragement along the way.

Our research shows that a work climate that rewards people based on their performance differentiates outstanding performance from average or poor performance. This helps to create engaged employees—those who are willing to put extra effort into improving their performance.

To increase your focus on rewards that motivate:

- Look for opportunities to praise good performance.
- Recognize and reward people on a timely basis for the level of their job performance.
- Reinforce outstanding performance.
- Ensure that recognition and encouragement greatly outweigh constructive criticism and negative feedback.
- Develop creative and flexible ways to recognize and reward individual and group performance.
- Celebrate individual, unit, department, division, and corporate accomplishments.
- Use the promotion system to help the best rise to the top.

The Third R: Respect

Effectively motivating the Millennial knowledge worker requires both individual and manager to enter into a behavioral contract in support of shared respect. While we all would like to embrace the golden rule of "treating others as you would like to be treated," a generational challenge appears to exist in this area. The following short discussion addresses this challenge and presents select strategies to address it.

From a review of Millennial literature and the Motivational Factors survey that shaped this book, it is quite clear that Millennials want to be treated as colleagues, they want their leader to have strong character, they want to work in an ethical environment, and they take pride in their work. Furthermore, there is research-based data to indicate that Millennials have respect for authority—as they have had for their parents and teachers. However, there are some generational differences that are not just behavioral differences, but critically important business issues.

Several authors address the motivation factor of respect. All have studied this challenge and made recommendations. In an effort to engage our reader/practitioner, I am presenting these recommendations in the form of a quiz. The following exercise is based on material appearing in *Generation Blend* by Rob Salkowitz and *Managing the Generation Mix: From Collision to Collaboration* by Carolyn A. Martin and Bruce Tulgan.

A Respect for Authority: Did You Know?

Directions: Indicate whether you were aware of the following respect factors.

	Yes	No
1. It's a curious paradox that the generation that questions everything is nevertheless more respectful of individuals and institutions who have earned their trust.	❑	❑
2. The track record shows that Millennials get along better with their parents, teachers, and much older workers than do Boomers or Gen Xers.	❑	❑
3. Many experts suggest that mentoring programs may be an especially effective way of integrating Millennials into the culture of the organization and bringing them up to speed on the formal and informal knowledge they need to be effective.	❑	❑
4. Millennials are well regarded by their elders, especially in the area of technology prowess.	❑	❑
5. Generational issues are important reflections of critical business matters that every organization is now experiencing as it transitions from the workplace of the past to the workplace of the future.	❑	❑
6. An organizational and managerial responsibility exists to create an environment that encourages courtesy, kindness, and respect.	❑	❑
7. Shared responsibility and mutual respect are exhibited through thoughtful, kind, and courteous behaviors.	❑	❑
8. Millennials claim that the relationship they have with their immediate boss is a critical factor in whether they stay or leave a job. They are certain at an early age about what they want that relationship to be.	❑	❑

As a manager, I can help further improve our "culture of respect" by:

___

___

___

Further Discussion

Shira Harrington, Director, Professional Search Positions, Inc.

It is a commonly accepted truism that people are motivated differently. In the case of Millennials, however, we should be encouraged to focus on the conditions under which a manager should feed this motivation through rewards. The author points out that many Millennials "believe they deserve a trophy, whether they win or lose." This is a recurring theme in generational literature that should be researched more intensively as Millennials move through management and beyond.

The author quoted Eric Chester, who noted that managers should "avoid heaping praise on minor task assignments that are a routine part of the job." While this seems like a simple enough concept, it should not be glossed over. For a generation that was given an "A for effort," recognition for simply showing up to work on time may be an expectation for some Millennials. Where does a manager draw the line in deciding what performance to reward? The author rightly suggests that we should "promote and reinforce excellence." Yet how does one define excellence for Millennials?

As the body of performance management literature evolves, we would benefit from a narrowly focused discourse on how to set clear expectations for Millennials that distinguish between minimum acceptable standards (not worthy of rewards) versus those behaviors that truly go above and beyond. While some managers may choose to reward the lowest common denominator, forward-thinking coaches will find a way to raise the bar to bring out the very best ingenuity from these young professionals. This competitive advantage will in turn serve the ultimate goal: to increase the bottom line.

Summary

This part focused on four key points. First, it identified those unique generational factors that influenced the importance of recognition, rewards, and respect as Millennial motivators. Second, it stressed the importance of appropriate recognition for the Millennial knowledge worker. Third, it presented concepts enabling the application of reward strategies. Fourth, it focused on strategies for developing a mutually beneficial climate in support of respect.

Part Seven: Learning, Training, and Technology now addresses the motivational importance that Millennials and their organizations place on the capacity to continually learn and remain competitive in a rapidly changing and fiercely competitive global economy.

PART 7

Learning, Training, and Technology

> ***"There is absolutely no question that America's economic leadership and the increasingly more competitive global economy will be influenced by the growing importance of our Millennial knowledge workers. 'Learning organizations,' 'managing human and intellectual capital,' and 'lifelong learning' are now common drivers of performance in any responsive organization."***
>
> **–Rick Humphress, Oracle Corporation**

In this part:

- ▶ Getting Started
- ▶ The Forces Shaping America's Economy
- ▶ Knowledge Has Become the Important Factor in Economic Life
- ▶ A Paradigm Shift From 20th-Century Training to 21st-Century Learning
- ▶ Millennials and Their Unique Learning Preferences
- ▶ Learning and Training Recommendations

Getting Started

The research that has led to writing this part positions the Millennial knowledge worker as a seminal force, a centerpiece, of the new economy. This strategic positioning of the Millennial knowledge worker is the result of a fortuitous combination of events. First, knowledge is the new wealth of organizations, and effectively managing this knowledge has become critical to our economic life. Second, technology has changed and will continue to change how we work. And this has also significantly altered the way we learn. In short, the knowledge economy has increased the importance of the learning organization. This dynamic has created the need for knowledge workers to learn faster and more effectively. Finally, the unique learning preferences of a generation that has "grown up digitally" directly support their comfort level with technology-mediated learning methods. The following four objectives support this assumption.

Research and Contributing Experts' recommendations resulted in this part's focus on the following four objectives:

- Understand the forces shaping America's economy and their implications for work and workers in the twenty-first century.
- Appreciate that knowledge has become the most important factor in economic life.
- Recognize that a paradigm shift from twentieth-century training to twenty-first-century learning has taken place.
- Recognize that unique Millennial learning preferences directly coincide with the rise of technology-mediated learning methods.

The Forces Shaping America's Economy

The importance of identifying strategies and tactics to motivate Millennial knowledge workers cannot be fully appreciated without understanding the forces shaping the American economy. Perhaps the best way to create an understanding of the forces—directly relevant to this book—is to examine select trends presented by authors Richard W. Judy and Carol D'Amico in the Hudson Institute publication *Workforce 2020: Work and Workers in the 21st Century.* Concepts from this publication—a sequel to the Hudson Institute's landmark study, *Workforce 2000*—establish an excellent platform for Part Seven.

Trends Shaping the American Economy

- **Rapid technological change as the seminal force influencing the American and global economy**

  The pace of technological change is accelerating. And in this rapidly changing environment there will be winners and losers among industries, companies, occupations, and individuals. This scorecard of "winners" and "losers" has taken shape faster than anyone imagined as the result of the global recession we are now experiencing.

  More specifically, rapid technological change alters the productive process, i.e., the way work is done, as well as the products themselves. And unlike the technological changes that underlay the earlier growth of assembly-line manufacturing that once increased the demand for unskilled labor, today's technological changes in America have tended to require more highly skilled workers, but fewer low-skilled ones. Enter the Millennial knowledge worker.

- **Further global integration of the U.S. economy**

  Global integration is the second force shaping the American economy, as documented in *Workforce 2020*. Quite simply, distance is no longer a communication challenge. By the late 1990s, the marginal costs of communicating globally via the Internet had plunged to zero for most users. Compared to the rest of the world, America enjoys a relative abundance of highly skilled workers in specialized sectors such as Information Technology. This is a global competitive advantage. Again, enter the Millennial knowledge worker.

▶ Diminishing monopolies and intensifying competition

The protection once provided by geography and the unavailability of satisfactory substitutes is fast disappearing for more and more producers. And as the Hudson Institute report states, "because companies face increasing competition, they must live with unrelenting pressure to become more efficient and respond quickly to changing technological and market conditions." To survive and thrive in the twenty-first century, individual Americans need to manage their most important assets—their workplace skills. Enter the career-driven Millennial knowledge worker.

▶ America's emerging high-tech and global economy

The Millennial knowledge worker is well positioned to respond to America's swiftly developing technologies, which will increase the demand for highly skilled and well-educated workers. Furthermore, as earlier portraits of Millennials have indicated, a profile of their important motivational factors makes them a perfect "behavioral fit" for a rapidly changing and more entrepreneurial economy that places a premium on adaptability and flexibility. Simply put, workers able to master technology and cope with change will have an advantage. Enter the Millennial, yet again.

▶ Implications for America's workforce

Becoming a productive worker in America's fast-paced, rapidly changing, technology-driven, globally competitive economy will not be easy. But the Hudson Institute's report, *Workforce 2020*, while not directed at Millennials, clearly positions Millennials as the perfect candidates to help shape America's economy. Quoting the report directly:

> ***"Workers will change jobs more often. Rapid change dictated by competitive pressures will force companies to evaluate their staffing needs constantly, which will lead to frequent 're-sizing' of their workforces. As a result, workers will change jobs, employers, and even occupations more often than in the past. Moreover, workers in all occupations will need to prepare themselves mentally and professionally for this uncertainty."***
>
> ***–Workforce 2020: Work and Workers in the 21st Century***

Once again, the Millennial knowledge worker appears well positioned for these changes.

Knowledge Has Become the Important Factor in Economic Life

The previous discussion establishes a framework for the importance of the knowledge economy and the compatible and important role of the Millennial knowledge worker in this economy. The following discussion goes a step further and reinforces the link between the knowledge economy, the emergence of the learning organization, continuous learning, and a new Millennial career model.

The Knowledge Economy, Organization, and Worker

Working with the assumption that knowledge has become the most important factor in economic life—the one indispensable asset of the organization—it is worth taking a moment to discuss each of the interrelated components. A select summary of key points presented by author Thomas A. Stewart in *Intellectual Capital: The New Wealth of Organizations* helps to establish the importance of understanding why "learning," "opportunities for growth," and "rapid advancement" are among the top Millennial motivational factors.

The Knowledge Economy

The case has been made, and will continue to be reinforced, that knowledge has become an organization's preeminent resource. Managing intellectual capital has become an organization's first priority. Thomas Stewart asserts that it is "more important than raw material, money, automobiles, oil, steel or any other products of the Industrial Revolution." The knowledge economy, often described as an Information Revolution, is currently driving the reinvention of business, economic life, and society. It has quickly become apparent that a new knowledge-based economy will require the need for new skills, organizational structures, management, and leadership strategies—and yes, new workers, knowledge workers, and even more specifically, Millennial knowledge workers.

The Knowledge Organization

Virtually every organization has become "information intensive." Organizations are dependent on knowledge as a source of what attracts customers and clients and as a means of running the place. According to Thomas Stewart's research, a "knowledge organization" is defined by three factors:

- The enormous growth in the sheer information it handles
- What the organization does with the information and how they use it to replace inventories, warehouses, and other physical assets, saving both money and time
- How knowledge-intensive organizations are structured differently than traditional companies.

An ultimate goal of the knowledge organization is to move beyond using knowledge to improve productivity in our old business—or doing the same with less. Tomorrow, the shift is in using knowledge as a form of competitive advantage—generating new business.

The Knowledge Worker

Thomas Stewart makes a simple yet critical point in stating, "the notion of a knowledge economy and a knowledge company has a bit of the abstract about them, but there is nothing abstract about 'knowledge.'" In the same way we have generated profiles of Millennials, we can also generate a profile of the knowledge worker—often our very same Millennial. Several characteristics of the knowledge worker follow:

- Information is the most important material used on the job.
- Information and knowledge are both the raw material of labor and its product.
- Knowledge workers experience an increase in the knowledge content of their work.
- Better-educated workers are being hired to perform knowledge-intensive tasks.
- The education premium provides the growing role of knowledge in creating value and wealth.
- Knowledge workers, alone or in teams, plan, organize, and execute many aspects of their own work.

While not all knowledge workers are Millennials, the previously presented profile directly parallels their employment and learning preferences.

This brief summary of the emergence of the knowledge economy, organization, and worker clearly creates a case that the Millennial knowledge worker, the fastest growing segment of our workforce, is well positioned to support the growth of the competitive economy.

An Organizational Assessment

Based on the previous profile of the knowledge economy, organization, and worker, briefly describe how you would assess your organization's strengths and areas needing more development for each factor.

Knowledge economy: ______________________________

____

____

Knowledge organization: ______________________________

____

____

Knowledge worker: ______________________________

____

____

The End of the Beginning

In the conclusion of her book, *Managing Knowledge Workers: The Skills and Attitudes to Unlock the Intellectual Capital in Your Organization*, Frances Horibe includes the statement quoted below. It not only summarizes the previous discussion, but sets the scene for the emergence of the learning organization.

> ***"Knowledge is now the coin of the realm, and the knowledge worker is the most important source of wealth in an organization. Companies are coming to terms with this and starting to assess how to leverage their intellectual capital. … [T]rying to introduce changes to use your intellectual capital to its best advantage is a daunting task. It will require not simply changing what we do but [also changing] what we think and how we relate to each other."***

The Emergence of the Learning Organization

During the past decade, an interesting commonality of interests has emerged between the academic and corporate communities—one that is a perfect fit for motivating the Millennial knowledge worker. Universities have embraced more business-like practices common to corporations. In fact, the explosive and successful growth of nonprofit universities has provided best-of-class models of applying business practices to education. Second, organizations—increasingly more knowledge driven—have launched their own "corporate universities" that enable the alignment of business and educational needs. And both universities and corporations have moved to competency-based, outcome-driven, and even employer-centric educational strategies.

Taking this a step further, we now talk, as part of our common vocabulary, about the "learning organization" and the "corporate university" as components of the responsive knowledge organization. This strategic approach to "just-in-time" and "on-the-job" "continuous learning directly parallel the Millennial motivation factors." "Growth opportunities," "learning," and "training/lifelong learning" were all in the top ten responses to the Motivational Factors Survey.

An entirely new Millennial mindset has emerged regarding not only "work and life" balance, but also "work and learning" balance. In short, learning must take place almost as a byproduct of people doing their work—in contrast to acquiring knowledge before performing a particular task.

Michael J. Marquardt, writing in *Building the Learning Organization*, presents a brief description of the "new learning organization." A brief organizational assessment based on Marquardt's book is presented for you to measure your organization's strengths as a learning organization. This is obviously a major recruitment and retention tool for Millennial knowledge workers.

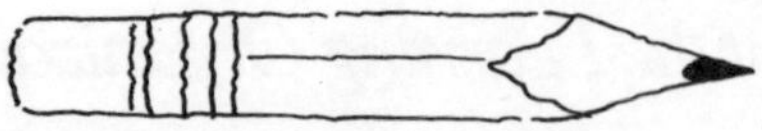

Is Your Organization A "Learning Organization"?

Review each of the following five characteristics of a responsive learning organization and identify your organization's current strengths and areas for development.

Current Strength	Should Improve	Characteristics
❑	❑	1. Learning is performance based (tied to business objectives).
❑	❑	2. Importance is placed on the learning process (learning how to learn).
❑	❑	3. The ability to define learning needs is as important as the answers.
❑	❑	4. Organization-wide opportunities exist to develop knowledge, skills, and attitudes.
❑	❑	5. Learning is part of work, a part of everybody's job description.

We can become a more effective learning organization by:

____

____

____

Implications of the Knowledge Economy and Learning Organizations for Millennial Knowledge Workers

Several positive characteristics quickly emerge from the previous discussion of the knowledge economy and the learning organization. These terms are a perfect match for meeting the Millennial motivational needs. They are "empowering," "sharing," "enabling," and "encouraging people to learn." Here is a short description of the importance of each characteristic as it relates to the Millennial motivational factor of learning.

Strategies to Address the Millennial Desire to Learn

Encourage Millennials to Learn: A common theme in almost every book on managing human and intellectual capital, workforce development, employee acquisition and retention, and the learning organization itself is that there is a new workplace competency. It is encouraging people to learn. This major motivational factor is most likely one of the reasons why your Millennials have joined your organization. It's not what the Millennial knows now but what they want and need to know for tomorrow. As Frances Horibe states, "To continue to create wealth through knowledge, people themselves must be up-to-date. Without a continual replenishment of the well of knowledge, it will eventually run dry."

In order for an organization to go beyond offering random training events and on-site college courses, it needs to consider establishing a formal, structured learning program for all levels of the organization. This program would include the following components:

- Formal training, learning, and development programs
- Encouraging informal learning
- Rewarding learning

Empower and Enable People to Learn: Perhaps one of the most effective sources of power a manager or leader can demonstrate is not "positional power," but "empowering others" to learn, take leadership, and assume responsibility for their projects and tasks. Empowering and enabling high-achieving, self-directed Millennial knowledge workers to learn offers a fluent extension of this process. It is also a direct fit for their motivational profile. While there are a wide variety of strategies to empower and enable people to learn, several that are especially relevant to knowledge workers appear below. How well does your organization do in meeting these learning needs?

The following strategies for empowering and enabling Millennials (or anyone) to learn are from *Building the Learning Organization:*

1. Institute personnel policies that reward learners.
2. Empower employees to learn and produce.

3. Balance the learning and development needs of the individual and [the organization.
4. Invite leaders to champion learning processes and projects.
5. Maximize learning from alliances and joint ventures.
6. Encourage leaders to model and demonstrate learning.

Encourage Knowledge Sharing and Demonstrations of Learning: One career commandment suggested by Michael K. Badawy, author of *Developing Managerial Skills in Engineers and Scientists*, is to delegate those things that you do best to allow time for you to learn new things. This delegation also allows you to monitor the performance of the individual to whom you delegate the assignment. Ironically, the opposite often happens in technology-driven knowledge organizations, where technical experts may hoard knowledge. One characteristic of the learning organization and managing of knowledge is establishing the strategy of learning from each other.

The New Millennial Career Model and Learning

An interesting confluence of the changing nature of work, worker, and learning has resulted in a new career model for the Millennial knowledge worker.

Earlier I referred to William Bridges' book *JobShift: How to Prosper in a Workplace Without Jobs.* More than ten years ago, he documented the disappearance of the regular concept of a 40-hour-a-week job with a routine day, familiar tasks and assignments, and actually "going to work" at a physical location. He talked about the changing and flexible nature of business needs that would require an equally flexible workforce.

In addition, instead of jobs, he suggested that projects have emerged as the predominant component of an organization's structure. And as many of us know, projects are usually time-limited and defined by parameters of schedule, budget, and quality. Leap forward ten years, and we see organizations responding to the needs of a rapidly changing, competitive global economy by embracing a project-driven model of organization and structural change. And this trend coincidentally parallels the Millennials' motivation needs for "flexibility," "growth opportunities," social interaction," "fast work cycle," and "changing and challenging work."

This book has drawn heavily from two separate but overlapping bodies of literature: understanding generational differences and appreciating the need to effectively manage knowledge workers. And Thomas A. Stewart formalizes the integration of these two disciplines in his book *Intellectual Capital: The New Wealth of Organizations*, in Chapter 12, "Your Career in the Information Age." The statements in the following exercise are from Stewart's book.

Career Strategies in the Information Age: A Checklist

Imagine that you're meeting with a new Millennial knowledge worker who is seeking guidance on how to manage his/her career in your organization. The Millennial is asking you to identify those strategies that would increase his/her knowledge of how to stay motivated and advance his/her career. Indicate which of the following strategies you would share with him/her.

- ☐ 1. "A career is a series of gigs, not a series of steps."
- ☐ 2. "Project management is the furnace in which successful careers are [forged]."
- ☐ 3. In the new organization, "[p]ower flows from expertise, not from position."
- ☐ 4. "Most roles in an organization can be performed by either insiders or outsiders."
- ☐ 5. "Careers are made in markets, not hierarchies."
- ☐ 6. "The fundamental career choice is not between one company and another, but between specializing and generalizing."
- ☐ 7. "Intellectual capital is the source of wealth for individuals as well as for organizations—and it is held in common between them."

I have selected the following strategies to coach my Millennials:

____

____

____

I would also add to the list of strategies the following career recommendation based on my own experiences as a manager:

____

____

____

A Paradigm Shift From 20th-Century Training to 21st-Century Learning

The paradigm shift from the "business of training" into the "business of learning" is not new to many of our reader/practitioners. From my experience working with our Contributing Experts, I am well aware that most organizations have made this shift. However, since publishing my book *Reengineering the Training Function: How to Align Training with the New Corporate Agenda* a number of years ago, I continue to find organizations that have not fully made this paradigm shift. It is a critical one to consider in meeting the Millennial motivational need of learning. The following is a brief summary of this concept from my book.

Traditional Corporate Perspective	The New Corporate Realities
Static or steady business and organizational development processes do not require an accountable and responsive training initiative.	Rapidly changing business trends directly impact organization and the need for continuous learning.
A traditional training department supports tightly focused HRD initiatives.	Training becomes one component of the Continuous Learning Organization.
Classroom-based, instructor-led training delivers limited courses in few locations on a regular basis.	Just-in-time competency-based training must now be available in diverse instructional formats and locations.
Little accountability for transfer of training and strategic impact on business and organizational development initiatives.	Considerable emphasis is placed on improving performance, return on investment through benchmarking, and continuous process improvement.

Ideally, we would like to work with the assumption that all organizations have moved in the direction of becoming responsive learning organizations. But classroom-based training is alive and "unwell" in many organizations. And the Millennials, as our new "digital natives," are the first to describe it as ineffective.

It quickly becomes apparent in the following discussion that organizations must change both pedagogical and methodological strategies. We recognize that this need for change is driven by a variety of factors, including the need to create a competitive workforce, employ new information technology learning systems, and generate return on investment. But perhaps an equally important driver of the need to improve our learning systems is the workforce itself—the Millennial knowledge workers. It would not be unrealistic to suggest that they are, at the very moment you are reading this page, participating in multiple social media networks, and blogs, Twitters, and tweets, and of course, Facebook or whatever happens to be the popular social media network at the time. Placing Millennials in a traditional classroom with notebooks and PowerPoint slides may be a fast track to the Help Wanted column.

Technology Changes Work

It is interesting to note that although we are currently enjoying the light-speed impact of new technologies changing how we work, the concept of technology in the workplace is not new. Books written about sociotechnical systems decades ago addressed the issues of how technology changes work and, as will be discussed in just a few pages, how it changes learning. In order to put this broader concept of technology changing work in perspective, a brief review of our critical assumptions is presented. The parallel to Millennial motivational needs is striking. The following short section is based on information appearing in *Sociotechnical Systems: A Source Book* by William A. Pasmore and John J. Sherwood.

Organizations as Sociotechnical Systems

In practice, working toward the joint optimization of the social and technological systems of an organization is a comprehensive process that requires a thorough understanding of an organization, including:

- The social processes that occur in organizations and the variety of theories and methods for making more effective use of human resources
- The technological processes used by the organization and the constraints that it places on the design and operation of the social system
- The theory of open systems, because no two organizations are exactly alike or are faced with the same environmental demands
- The mechanics of change, both in the execution of the initial sociotechnical system design and in provision for the continual adaptation of the organization to new environments.

Technological Changes in Work Parallel Millennial Motivators

An interest coalescing of technology and forces in human resources is taking place. These forces include the accelerating ways that technology has transformed work and the rapid growth of Millennial knowledge workers. While some technologies merely improve the existing ways of working, the emergence and widespread application of connected information work software is actually changing work itself. And as we briefly review four ways that technology changes work, we cannot help to think that these changes directly parallel the previous documented motivational needs of the Millennial knowledge worker.

The following list is based on material appearing in *Generational Blend* by Rob Salkowitz.

Four Ways Technology Changes Work

1. **Technology makes work collaborative.**

   The tools for collaborative technologies are, according to Rob Salkowitz, "getting better: more relevant, more contextual, less disrupting and better integrated into the information work environment." Interestingly, the Millennial motivational factors include "collaboration," "social interaction," "communities of interest," and "open communication with teams." These behavioral technology preferences directly parallel the Millennials' use of Blogger, LinkedIn, Facebook, and other Web 2.0 technologies.

2. **Technology collapses time and space.**

   As we know, appreciate, and even seek out for ourselves, technology has significantly redefined the concept of the workplace and workday. As Salkowitz points out, networked information and communication technology offers the ability to connect and secure voice and data networks anywhere and anytime, and provide a high-quality experience for accessing data, applications, and services. Coincidentally, our Millennial knowledge worker has clearly prioritized "flexibility" as the top motivational factor, followed by others relevant to communication technology, including "open communication with teams," "communities of interest," and "work and life balance."

3. **Technology makes work transparent.**

   Many of us remember, or are still experiencing, a work environment that requires going to the same place of work on a daily basis and working eight to ten hours under the physical supervision of a manager. For a number of reasons, especially the omnipotent presence of technology, the concept of the workplace has become—and will continue to develop into—a flexible and virtual relationship between employer and employee. Desks, file cabinets, and individual hard drives are no longer the home for reports, documents, and project updates.

   Organizations are now using Enterprise Resource Planning (ERP) systems and Manufacturing and Supply Chain Management systems to coordinate supply networks. In addition, the Internet, e-mail, text messaging, and voice mail have resulted in technology-based collaborative workspaces. And ironically, as Salkowitz points out, rather than having a boss physically watch over you, "the net result of these developments is that workers and their work products are more visible, accessible, and accountable than ever before." Transparency is now a face of the 21st-century workplace.

   And once again, coincidentally, Millennials who blog, Twitter, tweet, and manage their Facebook accounts find this new transparent work environment desirable, as it meets their bimodal needs. First, they do not necessarily take privacy for granted. Second, technology allows them to maintain compliance with organizational processes.

4. **Technology amplifies the potential of people.**

   When we reexamine the result of the Millennial Motivational Factors Survey and review the Portraits of Millennials, we find priorities placed on "career advancement," "challenging work," "treatment as colleagues," "social interaction," and "growth opportunities.

These motivational needs are now being met, in part, as connected information systems become smarter and more sophisticated. Several select attributes of the new technology amplify the potential of people, including small teams who can now perform tasks that previously required large numbers of people; more knowledge and job-specific functions will be embedded into software sharing information, previously limited and accessible only to experts. In addition, workers can visualize data in richer ways, and it pushes exceptional responsibility and competence onto the shoulders of our high-achieving Millennials.

Rob Salkowitz summarizes the implication of technology amplifying the potential of people as it specifically relates to Millennials in his statement, "What younger workers know is how to find information they need when they need it, using search engines, social networks, data visualization applications, and person-to-person communication tools." This combined new Millennial skill has been uniquely labeled "just-in-time comprehension."

Millennials in the Technology-Driven Workplace

It is important not to use "generational generalizations" to characterize each group and their attitudes towards technology and their learning style. However, there is a growing body of literature and research that describes Millennials not only as techno-savvy workers, but also as especially well suited to the needs of the new technology-driven workplace. The following checklist of Millennials' competitive advantages in the workplace is provided as a fluent transition to the final section of this part, "Millennials and Their Learning Preferences."

MILLENNIALS IN THE TECHNOLOGY-DRIVEN WORKPLACE: A CHECKLIST OF ATTRIBUTES

Research and Contributing Expert input have identified the following "technology attributes" that Millennials bring to the workplace. Identify which of the following best characterize Millennials that you supervise, and indicate if there are others that you would add to the list.

- ❑ 1. They have never known a life without a computer—through the use of technology, they can take in 20 hours of information in seven hours.
- ❑ 2. Millennials eagerly embrace technology in its many permutations and combinations.
- ❑ 3. They are independent and highly networked, both personally and technologically.
- ❑ 4. They are the first entirely technology-savvy generation to enter the workplace.
- ❑ 5. They appreciate continuous learning opportunities.
- ❑ 6. Technology is not an occasional tool, but a constant extension of themselves.
- ❑ 7. They want all the education that they can get on the job.
- ❑ 8. They excel at multitasking and building parallel careers—not focusing on one job at the exclusion of others.

CONTINUED

CONTINUED

- ❑ 9. They are accustomed to instant communication and long-distance collaboration.
- ❑ 10. Technology to them is a freedom. It is a tool that enables them to complete their jobs faster and easier.

Action Items:

The technology-driven attributes that characterize Millennials that I supervise are:

____

____

____

Other technology-driven attributes my team possesses include:

____

____

____

Millennials and Their Unique Learning Preferences

The following discussion serves as an internal summary, transitioning the reader into the final section of this part.

Millennials' Insatiable Appetite for Learning

Rick Humphress
Oracle Corporation

There is absolutely no question that America's economic leadership, in an increasingly competitive global economy, will be influenced by the growing importance of our Millennial knowledge workers. "Learning organizations," "managing human and intellectual capital" and "lifelong learning" are now common drivers of performance in any responsive organization.

More specifically, success at motivating the 21–30-year-old knowledge worker is anchored to three key drivers, presented by Contributing Expert Kitty Nix. First, Millennials are knowledge seekers with an insatiable appetite for relevant learning opportunities. Their loyalty is no longer anchored to their organization, but is anchored to their academic discipline and their very own knowledge portfolio, which they aggressively manage. Second, they seek continuous, just-in-time opportunities to learn and grow. Their learning preference is often on-the-job—having a need to learn what they need when they need it—and competency-based learning—relevant to their increasing their professional effectiveness. Third, while our emphasis is on the acquisition of knowledge, we should not overlook the importance of training, which provides a shorter-term solution to developing job-related skills. "Just-in-time" vs. "just-in-case" training is a critical Millennial motivational indicator.

An important component of developing learning organizations and human capital is technology. And the Millennial brings to the workplace "maximum" technology expectations as essential to their learning and career growth. As Contributing Expert Chris Ryan recommends, "an organization needs to provide the technological tools such as a laptop (that can be taken home for work after-hours), special software, instant messaging, and access to social networking websites. The Millennial knowledge worker is motivated by gaining access to new technologies as they become available to both keep their skills current and maintain their perceived 'edge' over the more senior coworker."

On-the-job sponsored learning and training and attractive office space with up-to-date technology and resources are now minimum requirements for motivating the Millennial knowledge worker.

Making a Case for Millennial Adult Learners: Coinciding Forces

There is a tendency to treat Millennial learners differently than other generational groups. This overlooks two key points. First, Millennials as digital natives are attracted to, and most comfortable with, technology-mediated methods of learning; yet these new learning technologies are of value to all generational cohorts. Second, in our enthusiasm to focus on Millennials' learning preferences, the key concepts of Malcolm Knowles's theory of andragogy—teaching adult learners—should not be overlooked.

Millennial as Digital Natives Gravitate to Technology-Mediated Learning

Rick Humphress states that a premise of this part is that learning should be different for the four broad sociological groups that include Traditionals, Baby Boomers, Gen Xers, and Millennials. However, he suggests that Millennials have unique needs associated with learning methods and the use of technology. In his research of adult learning theory, he has been unable to find a study that makes a distinction between adults based on age. Indeed, he argues, Knowles and others implicitly state that adult learning theory applies to all adults. From his perspective, his only meaningful differentiation between the various groups is the amount of life experience members of each group bring to training.

Even then, a Millennial could have more germane experience than a Baby Boomer depending on the area of inquiry. Therefore, it is apparent that the factors imputed to the Millennials are in fact important to all sociological classes, since they are important to all adults. In fact, Rick Humphress suggests that the trend to be noted is that the constantly changing knowledge economy has placed a premium on effective training for all workers. This has led to an improvement in technology-mediated learning methods for all users. It just happens to coincide with the rise of technology-focused Millennials in the workforce.

Malcolm Knowles's Theory of Andragogy: Assumptions

Anyone having the slightest experience teaching adult learners has formally or informally come to understand that adults learn differently than younger students. Knowles's theory of andragogy, discussed in his now classic book, *The Adult Learner*, addresses a variety of learning preferences that are relevant to all four generational groups.

- Adults need to know why they need to learn something before undertaking to learn it.
- Adults have a self-concept of being responsible for their own decisions, for their own lives.
- Adults come into an educational activity with both a greater volume and a different quality of experience than children do.
- Adults become ready to learn those things they need to know and to be able to do in order to cope effectively with their real-life situations.
- Adults are not subject-oriented but life-centered in their orientation to learning.
- Adults are motivated more by intrinsic motivators (self-esteem, job satisfaction, improved life quality, etc.) than by extrinsic motivators (bonuses, salary increases, promotions, etc.).

These concepts deserve our consideration as a platform to understand Millennial comfort with technology-mediated learning and with basic concepts of adult education.

Millennial Learning Preferences: Four Perspectives

A variety of educators and consultants have identified the unique learning preferences of Millennials. Each of the following four individuals offers specific observations and recommendations on how to support the Millennial motivational factor of learning. Let's begin with an academic perspective first.

A University and Research Perspective

Dr. Cathy Sandeen is Dean of Continuing Higher Education at the University of California-Los Angeles. In her article, appearing in the *Continuing Higher Education Review,* Vol. 72, 2008, she presents a comprehensive generational perspective on learning. It is entitled "Boomers, Xers and Millennials: What Are They and What Do They Really Want from Continuing Higher Education." It is a rigorously researched and well-documented article that addresses issues beyond the context of this book. However, there are two sections especially relevant to this part.

Based on her research and university administration and teaching experience, Sandeen draws the following conclusions:

- Boomers, Gen Xers, and Millennials are expert multitaskers and résumé-builders, and they are technology-immersed, networked, and connected.
- They are success-oriented and status conscious.
- Topics likely to appeal to them, in part, include new technology and basic job skills (presentations, finance, spreadsheets, career information).
- Because of their immersion in technology, they are likely to prefer distance learning.
- Due to their experience with traditional education, they continue to be drawn to classroom-based experiences as well.
- The opportunity to receive education via wireless devices is appreciated.
- They expect their educational experience to be highly customized.
- They expect 24/7 access to instructors and student services staff.
- Finally, and most interestingly, facilities that can create a Starbucks-like multitasking environment will be a big hit.

Millennial Learner Hypothesis: Program Selection, Format, Marketing

Dean Cathy Sandeen's research and analysis also generated a series of hypotheses about the needs or preferences of adult learners by generations. While you are encouraged to read her entire article for this broader perspective, those hypotheses which are specifically relevant to Millennial learners follow. Millennials will tend to:

- Show interest in career-related programs
- Show some interest in graduate school or degree preparation
- Prefer online formats over classrooms
- React positively to career relevance in marketing messages
- Appreciate the ability to sample a program prior to enrolling
- Show greater preference for electronic channels
- Show interest in social networking as a marketing channel

Not only have organizations moved out of "the business of training" and into "the business of learning," but they now find that they need to address both the learning preferences of Millennials and the challenges of teaching multigenerational audiences.

Learning Along with the Millennials

There is no doubt that organizations have embraced pedagogical and methodological concepts in the design and delivery of training. There is clear evidence that these changes have included moving beyond training as an activity—complete with small group activities, flipcharts, PowerPoint presentations, and refreshment breaks. And while globalization and information technology have, in general, improved training and education delivery, Russ Eckel, Founder and President, Nommos Group and Generations at Work, writing in his article "Learning Along with Millennials," makes a key point:

> ***"Important as these factors [globalization, information technology] are, there is another reason why almost all aspects of training [and education] must change—the workforce. To be specific, young workers, indeed the Millennials, have arrived. With them comes a whole new way of working and learning. Therefore, to understand your organization's future training [and education] needs lies in your understanding and integration of Millennial learning style."***
>
> **–Russ Eckel**

Russ Eckel introduces the concept of "Millennial modes of learning" by citing the work of Christopher Dede, a professor at Harvard University School of Education. He is an expert on learning technology and educational pedagogy. He identifies the following five elements, which together constitute the Millennial generation's preferred modes of learning.

Five Elements Constituting Millennial Modes of Learning

Identify which of the following elements you are currently using in your Millennial training and education programs. Also identify which element(s) you are not using, but should consider employing.

Currently Using	Should Consider	
❑	❑	1. Fluency in multiple media and simulation-based virtual settings
❑	❑	2. Communal learning involving shared experiential knowledge
❑	❑	3. A balanced amount of experiential learning, guided mentoring, and collective reflections
❑	❑	4. Expression through nonlinear associational webs
❑	❑	5. Co-creation of learning experience

Based on review of the previous listed five Millennial learning modes, I have identified the following strengths and areas for improvement:

____

____

____

When you compare the previously presented five elements constituting Millennial modes of learning with earlier profiles of Millennials, you can see a match between motivation factors and learning styles. Those behavioral characteristics included "multitasking," "being connected," "using a broad range of communication technology to share experiences," and "the desire to create their own learning experience." Learning for Millennials has more in common with their social networking practices, involving collaboration with friends, students, mentors, the ubiquitous presence of computers, and of course, an extraordinary array of technologies, now including vlogs (video logging) and microblogging (short blog posts under 140 characters).

Portfolio of Training Media

In the same way Millennials have moved away from developing traditional résumés and toward creating portfolios of life and work experience, their learning preferences gravitate toward a wide variety of training media. Russ Eckel, President Nommos Group and Generations at Work, credits Suzanne Roberts, a senior IBM learning specialist, with developing a wide portfolio of training media that constitutes the "Neo-Millennial Learning System." The mix of media includes:

- Self-study, Web-based training
- Mobile wireless courseware
- Web-based discussion groups
- Face-to-face workshops
- Online workshops

For those of us involved with graduate and certification programs for working professionals, we refer to this learning portfolio as "blended learning." This "Neo-Millennial" learning system also parallels the Millennial motivational factors presented earlier in the book. These include "state-of-the-art technology," "social interaction," and "communities of interest." The parallel between social networking and co-creating a shared learning experience is strikingly similar. Interestingly, major corporations are now encouraging and even requiring managers to actively engage in social networking as part of the organization's efforts in recruiting, managing, and motivating the workforce.

New Training Techniques Needed for Millennials

John Ambrose, Vice President of Strategy, Corporate Development and Emerging Business, Skillsoft, makes an important statement in his article "New Training Techniques Needed for Millennials," which sets the scene for his specific and relevant recommendations. He states:

> ***"Today's graduates—dubbed "Millennials"—are a completely new breed of workers compared with their predecessors. They have a different take on what makes a desirable work environment. The new generation coming into the workforce expects ongoing enrichment and challenges. We can't train this new generation the same way we did employees five or ten years ago."***
>
> **–John Ambrose**

He makes an important point that training (learning) will be seen as a benefit only if it is approached correctly. From his perspective as Senior Vice President of Skillsoft, he has the unique advantage of working with a wide variety of public- and private-sector organizations. And from this broad perspective he makes a number of recommendations that I have taken the liberty of presenting in the form of an organizational assessment.

MILLENNIAL LEARNER PREFERENCES & PRACTICES

Identify those Millennial learning practices that your organization is currently employing, and provide specific applications. Also, identify several Millennial learning practices that you are currently not employing but that have the potential to enhance your programs.

____ 1. Young professionals want to know that what they learn today will help them in their long-term career.

____ 2. Learning should be made part of the daily workflow rather than being relegated to training sessions that take them away from their jobs.

____ 3. New hires are accustomed to a very interactive digital lifestyle.

____ 4. Millennials, often described as "digital natives," are accustomed to receiving and disseminating information from multiple sources simultaneously.

____ 5. Millennials expect engaging learning experiences, whether they take place in the classroom or online.

____ 6. They presume that employers will communicate via highly produced, entertaining media.

____ 7. Millennials, raised on video games, gravitate toward multipath gaming techniques that put them in control.

____ 8. Virtual classrooms can be used to bring together groups of learners to interact and discuss topics that have been covered in online self-study.

____ 9. Interspersing multimedia learning that incorporates audio and video will keep their attention from waning.

____ 10. Millennials used to a 24/7 work and life balance can take advantage of digestible learning experiences on demand via mobile learning devices.

Even a quick review of the previous ten Millennial learning preferences and recommendations reinforces the importance for organizations to move continuous learning out of an isolated classroom, with PowerPoint presentations and printed handouts, and move to a learning platform that embraces the potential of podcasts, laptops, and MP3 players. "Learning anytime, anyplace, any way" is quickly replacing "just-in-case training."

Learning and Training Recommendations

This part has presented a broad variety of Millennial learning strategies and tactics. When employed, they will also lend support to the learning motivational needs of Millennials. A final set of recommendations is now presented by contributors to reinforce the application potential of these concepts.

Best-of-Class Practices

Rick Humphress
Oracle Corporation

- Scheduled training should be set so that it is more accessible to employees.
- Scheduled training should be revised to include more information germane to the employee's work setting and must elicit the learner's participation.
- Scheduled training should be taught by qualified trainers who understand the principles of adult learning and how to engage adult learners.
- Managers should have responsibility for the learning and development of their employees built into their job descriptions.
- Managers should have a subset of the adult learning skills demanded of training instructors.
- Managers should be evaluated on how well they develop the competencies of their employees.
- Organizations should provide and publicize learning centers (physical or virtual) that employees can access.
- Organizations should train employees on research methods to help them learn on their own.
- Organizations should actively "mine" employees for relevant data that can be placed in a data store that is available to all employees. One modern variant of this idea is the "wiki."

Checklists

The following steps should be taken in order to institute a learning environment that will meet the needs of all adult learners. The checklist items start at the highest strategy level and descend to the lowest tactical learning level:

- Do I have executive management support and direction? Executive management must establish a supportive environment for learning that encourages employees to participate and guides training in the task of providing learning and development.
- Have I engaged the learner in analysis? Instructional designers must involve the learners in the design of the training curriculum by forming planning committees or learning task forces.
- Have I empowered the learner to participate in the training? When analyzing the needs of a training program (using the ADDIE or some such model), you must be sure to leave room for an individual diagnosis of the needs of the particular learners attending each unique session of training.
- Have I aligned the course objectives with learner needs? Instructional designers and trainers must translate the competencies to be learned into a set of materials that will effectively transmit these competencies to the learner.
- Have I gathered learner-centric course evaluations? While Kirkpatrick, Philips, and others stress the financial impact of training programs, it is important to understand what personal value the training had for individual learners.

Learning and Training Recommendations

Kris Jensen, VP, Corporate Solutions
Wisdom Workers Solutions

Although the idea of lifelong learning was "pioneered" by Generation X, all generations have adopted their wisdom by recognizing that an employee's marketability hinges on lifelong learning. However, distrust in Corporate America's long-term promises by the youngest generations keeps them focused on short-term transactional arrangements. To enhance retention efforts, one top-twenty construction company opted to turn skeptics of long-term promises into committed employees by communicating a concrete picture of career potential with the firm. The company created a "womb to tomb" (entry level to senior executive) curriculum, tailored to each job group (i.e., Accounting, Project Management, etc.). A detailed role profile served as the foundation of the program, giving each employee a framework for their success on the job, including their job description, career path, training and development required, and business outcomes expected. These outcomes then became a clear set of measures by which to evaluate the employee's performance.

Competency models outlining the success factors required of leaders, managers, and employees provided a roadmap for training and development, and criteria for hiring and promoting employees, aligning individual talents and interests to the work. The curriculum outlined activities that would appeal to various learning styles and fit different locations and time availability. Managers and employees in each discipline confirmed the definition and scope of the jobs.

Additional programs were created to support employees as they progressed through their careers. A Peer Advisor program provided one-to-one on-boarding assistance by partnering one- and two-year employees with new hires to help them acclimate to the company and teach them the "unwritten" rules of the road, ultimately evolving into a longer-term mentoring relationship. An intensive, year-long leadership development program offered high-potential employees an entrée into high-performing upper management and executive levels. Designed to develop and maintain a pipeline of leaders for organizational sustainability, the program was based on the five prongs of the company's leadership competency model and included thought leadership in each component, along with hands-on practice in each competency area. Candidates were selected from the company's talent pool through formal talent reviews and succession planning processes.

Learning and Training Recommendations

Hector Velez, Executive VP, Business Development
HireStrategy

HireStrategy training program comprises the following elements: textbook training, quarterly company-wide training sessions, classroom training, and on-the-job (OTJ) training. Our program is designed as a road map to move our Associates into a successful career with HireStrategy as quickly and efficiently as possible.Several people contribute to our Associates' SmartStart training experience. SmartStart is facilitated by the Managing Director and others who may have responsibilities to familiarize new Associates with the HireStrategy environment. However, as they progress through each phase, they will recognize that, by design, they gradually take on greater responsibility for their own progress.

Starting a new job with a new organization is a critical time. We want our employees' transition into HireStrategy to be a positive experience with a positive outcome. After all, SmartStart exists due to the natural disorientation that comes from entering new surroundings. To assist new Associates, the Managing Director, and others who may help new employees settle into their new job, we designed checklists of actions and experiences to expose them to specific information, office layouts, equipment, hardware/software applications, work processes, and business systems important to their early development. These checklists are an integral part of our manual. Aside from guiding them through SmartStart, the process further integrates the new employees into the HireStrategy team.

Learning and Training Recommendations

Christopher R. Ryan, Deputy General Counsel
K12 Inc.

Technology is changing society and the work environment at a dizzying pace, especially for those who can remember work before e-mail or even computers. From its invention until the beginning of the 1990s, the personal computer was extremely expensive, making it unavailable for most users outside of an office environment or computer laboratory. Personal and work computers during this time were also not interconnected. This all changed with the advent of advances in technology, less expensive computers, and the commercialization of the Internet.

Today's Millennial workers represent the first group of workers who grew up in an Internet world. Indeed, the speed of change and pervasiveness of technology is second nature to them. As a result, businesses must support and nurture the need for Millennials to be "plugged in" and to have access to the technology they need to do their jobs. For example, a company I worked for gives employees the choice of a desktop or laptop computer. Millennials usually favor laptop computers because they provide flexibility in when and where work is performed. Instant messaging is a communication tool that some companies prohibit on their networks due to security and productivity concerns, but Millennials rely upon "IM" extensively to interact with others and fulfill their responsibilities. Another tool that Millennials rely upon to do their jobs is collaboration software, such as Microsoft SharePoint. Collaboration software enables users to post documents and comments asynchronously in a shared environment.

Staying current with technology is even becoming a necessary tool for attracting and interviewing Millennials. For example, the *Wall Street Journal* has reported on the increased use of the online virtual-reality platform "Second Life" as an interviewing tool with Millennials. Prospective employers invite candidates to meet them in a virtual office within Second Life, and each party selects an avatar to represent them in the interview. Today's employers must adapt and rise to the challenge of relating to and supporting Millennials' use of technology.

Further Discussion

Shira Harrington, Director, Professional Search
Positions Inc.

In the beginning of this part, the author quotes Frances Horibe, who makes a point that may be a touchstone in unlocking what triggers the Millennial knowledge worker:

> ***"Knowledge is now the coin of the realm, and the knowledge worker is the most important source of wealth in an organization. Companies are coming to terms with this and starting to assess how to leverage their intellectual capital."***

In recent years, the term "human capital" has become an "in" phrase among savvy business executives. In an attempt to describe the people part of the organization in a way which shows they are the key drivers to success, management may be treading on delicate waters when it comes to motivating their key knowledge worker Millennials, especially in the area of learning.

The question becomes, how do you integrate a company's need to build ROI with a Millennial worker's need for personal fulfillment, including learning and development? While an organization exists first and foremost to be profitable, with the lack of corporate loyalty in Millennials, any attempt to treat them as a number or a statistic may have the reverse effect of retaining them and making them feel like valuable, individual contributors.

This dichotomy is one that needs to be addressed in future research. It is true that engaged employees drive corporate capital; however, if Millennials feel that they are simply a data point in a human capital metric, they will be less motivated to participate in, let alone absorb, the learning that is needed to enhance their performance. At the end of the day, Millennials choose to engage in learning and development activities to enhance their own personal and professional development, not necessarily to drive corporate profits. Finding equilibrium between these competing objectives will determine how much Millennials allow their employers to leverage their human capital potential.

Summary

Part Seven had four key objectives. First, it explained that the forces shaping America's economy have implications for work and workers in the 21st century. Second, it stressed the importance of knowledge becoming the most important factor in economic life. Third, it documented that a paradigm shift from 20th-century training to 21st-century learning has taken place. Fourth, and finally, it demonstrated that the Millennials' unique learning preferences coincide with the rise of technology-mediated learning methods.

Part Eight: Pay for Performance takes on the challenge of demonstrating that an organization's efforts to meet the Millennial motivational factors discussed throughout the book will result a greater return on investment. It is the final piece of the human resource management continuum of recruiting, selecting, managing, motivating, and rewarding—not just with the previously presented "rewards and recognition" strategies, but with one of the Millennials' top motivators: money.

PART 8

Pay for Performance

> ***"Flexible pay-for-performance initiatives that can be implemented and adapted to shorter time frames—12, 24, or 36 months, very much like emerging prenuptial agreements—are now needed for Millennial knowledge workers."***
>
> **–Rick Humphress, Oracle Corporation**

In this part:

- Getting Started
- Money as a Driver of Superior Performance
- Beyond the Performance Appraisal
- Identifying Strategies for Providing Financial Rewards for Knowledge
- A Pay-for-Performance Initiative

Getting Started

This part focuses on four objectives. Contributing Experts have provided pay-for-performance strategies that enhance the relevance and application of the following four objectives.

- Seize the opportunity to build on the foundation of intangible rewards and recognition motivators presented in Part Six to now include the tangible motivator of money as a driver of superior performance.
- Move beyond the traditional concept of a performance appraisal in order to implement a pay-for-performance system.
- Identify and employ strategies for providing financial rewards for knowledge.
- Implement a pay-for-performance system in shorter time frames of 12, 24, or 36 months.

Money as a Driver of Superior Performance

Part Six: Rewards, Recognition, and Respect focused on four key points. First, it identified those unique generational factors that influence the importance of recognition, reward, and respect as Millennial motivators. Second, it stressed the importance of appropriate recognition for the Millennial knowledge worker. Third, it presented concepts enabling the establishment of an organizational and managerial climate to apply reward strategies. Fourth, it focused on developing a mutually beneficial climate in support of respect.

Examples of the importance of Millennial knowledge worker reward, recognition, and respect strategies selected from Part Six include:

- The Millennial age cohort places considerable importance on the motivational factors of recognition, reward, and respect.
- Millennials are drawn to organizations and managers that offer frequent recognition.
- When Millennials' need for recognition is met in a timely and authentic manner, they go to the next step and exceed normal expectations.
- Millennials have a set of clearly defined reward expectations, including increased responsibility, opportunities to learn, and frequent praise and feedback for performance.
- Effectively motivating Millennial knowledge workers requires both individual and manager to enter into a behavioral contract in support of respect.

Money as a Motivator

Money is not a prime motivator, and in most cases, it starts to lose its value as a motivator at a certain point. However, when tied to a well-designed pay-for-performance system and comprehensive benefits package, it meets a variety of Millennials' tangible and intangible motivational needs.

Most experienced managers and human resources professionals know that money is one of the most short-lived motivators. We also know that it does not have as much power to attract and retain Millennial knowledge workers as many think it does. However, money is an important part of a balanced portfolio of reward strategies. In a survey commissioned by Robert Half International and Yahoo! HotJobs, with results published in *What Millennial Workers Want: How to Attract and Retain Gen Y Employees*, respondents ranked salary as 9.5 in importance on a 1-to-10 scale, with 10 being the most important. An opportunity exists to build on the foundation of intangible rewards and recognition to now include the tangible motivator of money as a driver of superior performance.

Beyond the Performance Appraisal

To implement an effective pay-for-performance system, you need to go beyond the traditional concept of a "performance appraisal." The implementation of an effective pay-for-performance initiative, designed to meet the needs of the Millennial knowledge worker, requires a systems view of performance management. This includes building upon a foundation of reward, recognition, and respect; going beyond traditional performance appraisals; and, finally, rewarding knowledge.

The knowledge and experience of Contributing Expert Peter W. Kennedy, Principal, PRM Consulting Group, and his associate, Sandy Grogan Dresser, are now drawn upon to address this challenge. Their discussion sets the scene for this part's discussion of pay for performance. Their contributions to this chapter have been selected from articles that they wrote for the *Compensation of Employee Benefits Journal,* which is no longer in print.

Appraising and Paying for Performance: Another Look at an Age-Old Problem

Peter W. Kennedy, Principal
PRM Consulting Group

Why is the relatively simple notion of improving performance through management and appraisal so difficult to successfully implement in practice? The reasons are unfortunately numerous enough to consume entire textbooks on the subject. For the most part, however, they relate to simple human weaknesses: fear, pride, impatience, lack of candor or discipline, procrastination, and poor communication skills. But most of all, even reasonable people don't necessarily agree. We simply don't come to the business at hand with the same expectations; each of us brings with us our own set of values and beliefs, with resulting differences in what we deem acceptable, outstanding, marginal, or dare I say, just plain old good.

The most common complaints are that appraisals:

- Take too much time
- Are too subjective
- Are all the same
- Make distinctions without a real difference
- Are not timely enough
- Belittle people
- Ignore the system
- Are used for too many purposes which often conflict

The purpose of this part is not to instruct our readers on how to address and resolve each of the previously listed performance appraisal complaints. Rather, it is to suggest that few would disagree with the contention that performance appraisals have been, for the most part, a resounding failure in corporate America. Surveys indicate, time and again, the widespread dissatisfaction with formal, written performance appraisals, both for employees who are subjected to the annual ritual and for the supervisors who are required to conduct them.

Other Approaches to Consider

The widespread dissatisfaction with traditional appraisals and merit pay has spawned a number of alternative approaches, which are not necessarily mutually exclusive. Each has its own advantages and disadvantages. Success with any single approach depends on an organization's ability to articulate and stick to the approach's central purpose and then implement and maintain it consistently over time.

Management by Objectives (MBO)

A common component of what we consider to be a traditional performance appraisal, MBO is worth mentioning not only because it remains widespread, but also because it explicitly recognizes the need for performance planning, not just appraisal. Where work is not routine, MBO can be and is used by supervisors, in consultation with those they supervise, to establish worthwhile and meaningful work goals at the beginning of the year. Performance is then appraised at the end of the year, based on how well the goals were achieved.

If done correctly, MBO helps to control the element of surprise in year-end appraisals, gives employees some constructive influence over what is to be appraised, and is more likely to result in a common understanding and agreement as to what was actually achieved at year end.

Total Quality Management (TQM)

W. Edwards Deming called performance appraisal one of the seven deadly diseases. Among other criticisms, he indicated that the traditional performance appraisal discourages risk-taking, leaves people depressed and bitter, and is unreliable and inconsistent as a measurement tool.

Deming's prescription for total quality management is to get rid of performance appraisals altogether. Instead of grading everyone, the organization should emphasize pride in workmanship and treat everyone the same within certain control limits. The call to abandon the formal performance appraisal as we know it in the name of total quality management and improvement is compelling given the success of Deming's methods.

Multi-Source Assessment

Where Deming's clear goal is the improvement of company performance through the careful management of product quality, the focus in multi-source assessment (or 360-degree feedback) is on obtaining a more complete understanding of all of the employee's performance successes and setbacks by getting feedback from as many people who interact with the employee as possible. Rather than getting just one assessment from the direct supervisor, organizations that use multi-source assessment typically find the aggregate result to be more a more thorough and therefore more accurate and reliable assessment of individual performance.

A typical approach might involve six to ten raters for each person. Finding enough individuals familiar with each person's work can be a problem, unless work is very much centered in teams. A similar issue can be the selection of the raters. A good management information system is necessary to report and administer the multiple ratings. Raters can be trained to develop their rating abilities; the rating results can be used to provide feedback on rating consistency.

Assessing Individual Competencies

While definitions of the term may vary, the basic concept of a competency is any individual attribute that can help ensure organizational success. Competencies include knowledge, skills, abilities, behaviors, other personal attributes, or even values that people bring to their work. The term is intentionally broad so as to capture important personality traits, such as integrity, initiative, optimism, energy, and honesty.

The rationale for including competencies in performance appraisals is that they build a stronger, more flexible workforce driven by customer focus, guided by a global competitive strategy, focused on learning as a competitive advantage, and supportive of worker mobility within and between companies. Each of these rationales is especially relevant to motivating the Millennial knowledge worker.

Identifying Strategies for Providing Financial Rewards for Knowledge

This book is not just about motivating Millennials, but is more specifically about Millennial knowledge workers. This raises the bar for identifying motivational strategies to address the specific motivational needs of knowledge workers as they relate to pay for performance. More specifically, the following brief discussion acknowledges the need to:

- Identify organizational processes that reward intellectual capital
- Implement systems capable of managing intangible assets
- Develop flexible compensation and benefits systems

Identify Organizational Processes that Reward Intellectual Capital

There is no doubt that an ever-growing percentage of individuals are now described as "knowledge workers." In simplest terms, this means that information and knowledge are the raw materials of their labor and its products. This had led to the concepts of a "knowledge economy," a "knowledge organization," and an organization's "intellectual capital."

Thomas A. Stewart, writing in *Intellectual Capital: The New Wealth of Organizations,* states that "Every organization houses valuable intellectual materials in the form of assets and resources, tacit and explicit perspectives and capabilities, data, information, knowledge, and maybe wisdom." Intellectual capital is strategically located in an organization's people, structure, and customers.

Paying for Intellectual Capital

There is no question that intellectual capital is a valuable asset to an organization. In simplest terms, smart workers work smarter. There is documented evidence that a relationship exists between a worker's education and productivity. However, Thomas Stewart raises an important point, especially relevant to motivating Millennial knowledge workers: Organizations and managers have had a hard time distinguishing between the cost of paying people and the value of investing in them.

Tools for Measuring and Managing Intellectual Capital

The following assumptions suggest the need to identify tools and processes that reward knowledge workers.

- The number of knowledge workers—a large percentage, Millennials—is rapidly increasing.
- A need exists to not only attract and recruit Millennial knowledge workers, but also identify strategies to motivate, retain, and develop them.
- There is a difference in the cost of paying people and the value in investing in them.
- A need exists to identify tools to measure human capital.

Thomas A. Stewart concludes his book, *Intellectual Capital*, with a variety of strategies and tools to measure and manage intellectual capital. As one example, he indicates that while answering the following questions won't yield quantitative data about human capital, it will yield a rich harvest of qualitative information.

Human Capital Measures

Answer and discuss each of the following questions with your colleagues. Identify the measurement tools that your organization is currently using as well as those that need to be implemented.

1. Among the many skills possessed by your employees, which do customers value most? Why?

2. Which skills and talents are most admired by your employees? What accounts for any difference between what customers value and what employees value?

CONTINUED

CONTINUED

3. What emerging technologies or skills could undermine the value of your proprietary knowledge?

4. Where in your organization do high-potential managers most want to be assigned? Where do they least want to work? How do they explain their preferences?

5. What percentage of managers has completed plans for training and developing their successors?

6. What percentage of all employees' time is spent in activities of high value to customers? What percentage of expert employees' time is spent in activities of low value to customers?

7. When competitors are hiring, do they hire from you?

8. Why do people leave you to accept jobs elsewhere?

CONTINUED

CONTINUED

9. Among experts in your labor market—including headhunters—what is your company's reputation vis-à-vis its competitors?

____

____

____

Application Exercise: Based on your answering and discussing each of the previous questions, identify the following.

A current measurement our organization is using: ____________________

____

____

A measure that we need to implement: ____________________

____

____

Flexible Compensation and Benefits

There is common agreement among economists, business leaders, and politicians that the driver of success in "The New Economy" is knowledge. The demand for knowledge workers is great and growing, with an estimated 60 percent of all jobs now knowledge-based. Those organizations that survive and thrive in a fiercely competitive global economy will have to rethink their workforce strategies and transform their management and human resource practices to attract, retain, engage, and develop workers of all ages.

However, the Millennial offers a special challenge. In particular, the Millennial knowledge workers realize that they are an attractive commodity in the competitive labor market and have demonstrated the ability to effortlessly job-hop for better opportunities. In order to meet their motivational needs, as addressed in previous parts, organizations need to provide not only innovative learning opportunities and flexible work arrangements, but also creative and responsive compensation and benefits programs. "Pay for performance" quickly emerges as a driver of this employee attraction, engagement, and retention strategy.

A Pay-for-Performance Initiative

A pay-for-performance initiative, implemented in shorter time frames of 12, 24, or 36 months, is required to effectively motivate Millennial knowledge workers. Before the presentation of pay-for-performance motivational strategies, the following two important assumptions must be examined. They are especially relevant to Millennials. First, a human resources professional will quickly suggest that the behavior that is recognized and rewarded is the behavior that is repeated. Second, as stated earlier in this part, a survey commissioned by Robert Half International and Yahoo! HotJobs found that employees ranked salary as 9.5 in importance on a 1-to-10 scale. In short, while all previously discussed Millennial motivators are important, let us not overlook money.

Paying for Performance: An Overview

Rick Humphress
Oracle Corporation

We begin by addressing and responding to a variety of assumptions necessary to establish a relevant pay-for-performance system. This includes, in part, removing politics and "perceptional" elements from reward systems and instead having rewards linearly tied to performance. In addition, a comprehensive benefits package will provide opportunities to customize financial motivators for not only Millennials, but a variety of age cohorts. In many cases, generous time off and flexible schedules in support of work/life balance carry as much weight as competitive salaries.

Many Millennial knowledge workers have experienced mergers, acquisitions, and significant organizational changes. Products and services have been outsourced, insourced, or simply eliminated. As a result, Millennials have become behaviorally conditioned to perceive themselves as replaceable and driven by competitive market conditions. Flexible pay-for-performance initiatives that can be implemented and adapted to shorter time frames—12, 24, or 36 months, very much like emerging prenuptial agreements—are now needed.

Best-of-Class Practices

In order for a pay-for-performance system to be effectively implemented, the following conditions must be met. These conditions flow from Vroom's Expectancy Theory Model, discussed below.

- ▶ Employees trust management.
- ▶ Management has implemented a valid job evaluation system.
- ▶ Management has established clear performance factors.
- ▶ Management adequately funds the system.
- ▶ Management has implemented an accurate appraisal system without forced distribution models.

Consider pay for performance as one of a number of coordinated efforts rather than as a single silver bullet for increased performance. Research literature cannot identify a single pay-for-performance system implemented as the sole solution for improved productivity that has ever succeeded.

Checklist

Pay-for-performance perversions to eliminate:

- ❑ Too much focus on the short term at the expense of the long term. If your pay-for-performance plan sacrifices the long term for short-term benefits, it may fail to achieve the desired results.
- ❑ Setting limits on expectations encourages mediocrity. If your pay-for-performance plan defines minimal expectations too low, it may erode overall performance.
- ❑ Too much emphasis on the individual destroys teamwork. If your pay-for-performance plan rewards the individual without recognizing the role of the team, it could discourage collaboration.
- ❑ Too much internal competition reduces productivity. If your pay-for-performance plan pits individuals against one another for scarce rewards, they may engage in counterproductive activities that improve their changes for reward—but not organizational effectiveness.

The Vroom Expectancy Theory

Pay for performance will work only if each of the following causal links is strong:

1. Employees attach value to the desired result of higher pay (valence).
2. Employees believe that rewards will actually be provided as a consequence of high performance (instrumentality).
3. Employees believe that they can actually accomplish the task that will lead to the reward of higher pay (expectancy).

The ASPIRE Model

Motivating people through higher pay is only one of several methods for improving worker performance. The ASPIRE human performance improvement model identifies five factors:

- **Actuate** — Understand how positive and negative motivators affect worker performance.
- **Skills** — Analyze, design, develop, implement, and evaluate training solutions to increase worker performance.
- **Power** — Understand how job design affects an individual's ability to perform the job.
- **Information** — Understand the design of process documentation and job aids (employee performance support systems) for improved worker performance.
- **Resources** — Identify and quantify the gaps in the deployment of necessary resources, tools, and environmental support.
- **Expectations** — Understand how such factors as self-esteem, work ethic, values, and quality orientation affect job performance, in order to better match the worker to the work being performed.

Millennial Expectations: Compensation and Benefits

Money can take on a variety of forms within an organization's compensation system. In simplest terms, it is thought of as salary. However, it can also include bonuses, profit sharing, incentive programs, and even stock options. However, while too often it is thought of as the major source of employee satisfaction, it is only one component of how an organization rewards its employees. In addition to money, many organizations have a full range of employee awards programs. Finally, the human element in the personal touch, ranging from a simple pat on the back to public and private praise, completes the reward equation. Frances Horibe, in *Managing Knowledge Workers,* sums it up in stating, "When the money is taken for granted and the plaques gather dust, these [personal touches] are remembered. It is a powerful motivator in and of itself and gives meaning to the money and the awards."

Money as a Means to Freedom

Both the formal Motivational Factors Survey and a review of Millennial literature generated similar conclusions. The very same generational cohort that wants "fun and social interaction," "flexibility and work/life balance," and "recognition, respect, and rewards" also wants security, compensation, and benefits. What may initially appear a bimodal set of wants quickly becomes clear when Millennial priorities are examined.

When we examine Millennial priorities of wanting greater integration between work and life at the workplace, the desire to develop portable skills, a concern with making a difference in the community, environment, and world, money becomes a means to an end. More specifically, Millennials view money as a means to achieve freedom, to have a choice about their lifestyle and when and where they work.

Paying for Performance: Implementation Challenges and Leadership

To be successful, pay for performance requires the organization, human resources professionals, and managers to address and overcome a variety of challenges. Presented quotes from Peter Kennedy's article "Appraising and Paying for Performance: Another Look at an Age-Old Problem" help to put the challenges and opportunities into perspective.

Pay-for-Performance Challenges

Peter W. Kennedy
PRM Consulting Group

The Zero-Sum game

In order to fully understand the issue of paying for performance, we must first recognize that money is a limited resource. In a typical zero-sum game, one individual's gain is another's loss. Most pay-for-performance systems have this unfortunate attribute, at least to some extent. Merit pay, which always purports to pay for performance by determining salary increases based on performance appraisal results, is almost always doomed by this fundamental constraint.

Plain old recognition, with no monetary component, has no such constraint. Its supply is essentially unlimited. Paying for performance sets up winners and losers. Recognizing performance, on the other hand, is purely win-win.

Motivation and Money

If performance appraisals do not seem to motivate people, but recognition does, what about money? Well, let's try to be reasonable about the response: of course it does! But only to a point.

Aon Consulting used to conduct an annual study titled "United States@Work," which correlated numerous variables to a set of six questions intended to reflect employees' commitment to the organization: pride in the work (willingness to refer company's products and services or the company itself as a place to work); productivity (ability and desire to work with others); and tenure (predisposition to leave, and how much of a pay increase this requires). Pay, as a driver of commitment in these studies, is consistently ranked high, but not in the top ten factors that respondents say is most important in reinforcing their commitment to their employer.

[This is in contrast to other survey results, such as the Millennial Motivation Factors Survey, which found pay for performance ranked within the top ten, and the previously cited Robert Half International survey, which ranked money as 9.5 on a scale of 1 to 10.]

Some critics of pay-for-performance systems have pointed out that money, in and of itself, particularly when tied to the achievement of particular goals, can have the effect of redirecting one's attention away from the task at hand to the monetary incentive to be gained. In other words, the acquisition of money becomes the end in itself, sometimes to the detriment of the work itself, even possibly degrading the quality of work and/or encouraging purely self-serving individual behavior. This observation became abundantly clear in the fall of 2008 as the financial sector collapsed but many executives were paid handsome bonuses that encouraged overly risky behavior.

The Element of Surprise

Which leads to a crucial, but often overlooked point: money is more effective when it is used as a reward rather than an inducement. Reward, in the meaning intended here, is a retrospective assessment and acknowledgement (with a significant monetary value). It is most effective when there is an element of surprise. It is the unanticipated award that tends to reinforce behavior and results without detracting from one's interest in the work at hand.

Performance Appraisals and Pay

So, should performance appraisals be tied to pay? In my opinion, they should provide information that leads to basic decisions over time about which employees to terminate, retain, or promote. They should not be used to make miniscule distinctions in pay adjustments. Let's keep the focus of performance appraisals squarely on simple communication about what needs to happen on the job.

Courage and Commitment

Sue McLeod, Senior Consultant
Hay Group

Why worry about paying for performance? Our research shows that the #1 reason for voluntary attrition of high performers is compensation. And you do want to keep your high performers, don't you? Think your Millennials (and other employees) won't find out where they stand compared to their peers? Think again. Remember, this is a generation that is highly connected, thinks they should have access to all important information, and shares with people they barely know.

How do you know if your compensation truly pays for performance? There are two simple tests:

- Do your highest performers consistently receive significantly higher rewards?
- Do your poorest performers consistently receive the lowest rewards?

Your managers are the front line of your pay-for-performance system. They need courage and commitment to succeed.

- Share your commitment. Give managers the tools they need to make tough decisions, communicate consistently, and send the right messages about superior performance.
- Bolster their courage with training, coaching, and support.
- Keep the focus. Measure results and give managers feedback and more training or coaching if needed.

Internal Freelancers and Spot Bonuses

Neil Sawyer, Senior Director, Human Resources
The Campagna Center

Older workers probably grew up with the philosophy instilled in them that they must give their life to the company, and for whatever the company gives them back, they should be grateful. Young workers don't seem to have this presumption. They expect to be paid for work done and are not shy about asking for it.

Freelancers

Most leading publishing companies I am familiar with make use of internal freelancers. These are regular full-time staff members who contract to do work in other departments or divisions of the company on their own time. These are employees who usually have a valued, specific skill set and are typically younger and more eager to get extra money. The company benefits because the excess work would have to be farmed out to a contractor, or temp help would have to be brought in to complete it. Having an employee do the work gives a sense of corporate insider knowledge that is often valuable and can actually decrease the amount of time it takes to get an assignment done. All work to be freelanced in-house must be approved in advance, and a rate of pay that would be higher than the hourly wage of the employee but less than a contractor must be agreed upon. This work must be done at home and not with company equipment—a requirement that younger employees don't mind.

Spot Bonuses

The same organization uses another form of payment for piece work. This is the use of "spot bonuses" for employees who contribute in a significant way to a major project or who have gone above and beyond their normal duties for an extended period of time. These bonuses can range from $500 gross to $5000 net, depending on the scope of the particular project.

Further Discussion

Shira Harrington, Director, Professional Search Positions, Inc.

In his checklist of "pay-for-performance perversions to eliminate," Rick Humphress points out two related issues that should be expanded upon in future research and writing. He notes, "Too much emphasis on the individual destroys teamwork," and "Too much internal competition reduces productivity." As we contemplate ways to motivate Millennials, more consideration needs to be given to the value of rewarding the group, beyond the individual contributor.

Most Millennials were raised in a culture that rewarded teamwork. From "No losers in Little League" to being given group projects throughout their schooling, Millennials appreciate the value of teamwork more so than most generations. As a result, many are more motivated when they know that their team has done a good job and moreover, when rewards are fair.

Equity is a concept that is not lost among this generation, which often wants to equalize rewards rather than recognize the lone superstar. While certainly the latter motivation exists, employers will find that a team-based, project-based reward system, in conjunction with a well-designed individual-based performance plan, will go a long way to building a sense of cohesion and, dare I say, family among this peer-seeking cohort. Sharply contrasted with the motivators of their elder siblings, Generation X, which often seeks rewards for individual entrepreneurial prowess, Millennials will frequently flock toward collaborative achievement. As Millennials continue to grow into the ranks of management, performance measures are likely to evolve into an appreciation of the power of "we" versus "me."

Summary

Part Eight's objectives focused on four key points. First, an opportunity exists to build on the foundation of intangible rewards and recognition motivators presented in Part Six to now include the tangible motivator of money as a driver of superior performance. Second, in order to implement an effective pay-for-performance system, organizations must go beyond the traditional concept of a "performance appraisal." Third, strategies for providing financial rewards for knowledge were identified. Fourth, a pay-for-performance initiative, implemented in shorter time frames of 12–36 months, is required to effectively motivate Millennial knowledge workers.

APPENDIX

Appendix Overview

Motivating the Millennial Knowledge Worker has been designed as both a resource for the individual reader and a classroom training manual. This Appendix provides reader and trainer with further application resources.

The first section outlines suggestions for implementing your action plan. It continues with the book's Contributing Experts identifying and addressing specific Millennial motivational changes. It concludes with a Chapter Checklist: Designing Your Action Plan.

The second section provides a unique organizational assessment tool. The TIP'M© Methodology, developed by Contributing Expert Mark Steffanina, provides both tactical and strategic approaches to building a pro-Millennial workplace by using the Team Improvement and Prioritization Matrix©. Further information about the implementation of this copyrighted tool is available from the author.

Implementing Your Action Plan

Motivating the Millennial knowledge worker is not a passing human resources management fad. Rather, it is now a workforce necessity for organizations seeking to respond to an increasingly more competitive global marketplace, economic challenges, and rapidly changing technologies. Earlier in this book, Millennials were described as the fastest growing segment of the workforce. Further defining this population to focus on Millennial knowledge workers—those individuals who use their heads more than their hands to produce value—identified a segment of the workforce that will drive America's New Economy. As previously quoted, Neil Howe and William Straus describe the impact of the Millennials this way: "This rising generation will introduce itself to the nation and push the nation into a new era." A need has emerged for highly interactive "performance partnerships" between Millennial, manager, and human resources professional.

This appendix presents three application tools for reader and trainer:

- An opportunity is presented to review Contributing Experts' final recommendations addressing specific Millennial motivational challenges.
- A review of each part's learning objectives is presented in a checklist format, allowing the reader to identify those specific behaviorally based Millennial motivational challenges relevant to their workforce.
- A motivational factors survey is introduced, providing readers with an opportunity to implement an organizational Millennial motivational assessment.

Millennial Motivational Challenges: Expert Strategies

Over twenty Contributing Experts have been involved with this book from start to finish. It is appropriate to include examples of how they have addressed specific Millennial motivational challenges. Our experts' biographical sketches appear in the Introduction of the book.

The Importance of the Generational Perspective

Jennell Evans, President and CEO
Strategic Interactions, Inc.

The North American workplace today is the most age-diverse workforce that we have known since the Industrial Revolution. At no other time in history have so many and such diverse generations worked together side by side. There have been multiple generations in the workforce before, but the organizational hierarchy of the manufacturing economy mostly segregated them from one another.

Today, those social and physical separations exist to a much lesser extent. The new, flatter organizational structures and the need for teamwork are creating a generational mix that we have never experienced before, with four generations now in the workforce. This remarkable mix of perceptions and values can foster incredible creativity or, if not managed properly, can lead to intergenerational conflict and high turnover.

To motivate Millennials, the youngest of the four generations in the workforce, leaders of organizations will benefit by cultivating the following two strategies:

1. Embrace social responsibility from the top down:

    - Organizations that authentically and visibly "walk the walk" on social responsibility will attract, engage, motivate, and retain Millennial talent. In 2007, Deloitte & Touche USA conducted a survey and found that two-thirds of the 18- to 26-year-olds responding said that they would prefer to work for companies that allow them to contribute to nonprofit organizations.
    - Since 86% of all U.S. high schools provide community service experiences, Millennials enter the workforce understanding how they can have a positive impact by doing something they feel passionate about, and this is very important to this generation of workers.
    - With the highest rate of volunteerism ever in the U.S., employers who embrace social responsibility as a core value will not only attract "the best and the brightest," but will most likely be better positioned to retain this talented generation and create a pipeline of future leaders.

2. Embrace diverse work/life balance strategies.

    Millennials are committed to work/life balance, and for many, that balance includes opportunities to do things other than work, and to connect with people through volunteer activities, which become part of their identity and their social networking in person and online.

Don't Stereotype Us!

Erin Nicole Gordon, Systems Integration and Technology
Accenture

Contrary to the plethora of negative stereotypes surrounding the twenty-something young professional, Millennial knowledge workers can be successfully motivated. By identifying common attributes (including independent or do-it-yourself, engaged, ambitious, innovative, and compassionate) and successfully providing opportunities that engage these attributes in the workplace, an employer can retain and fully realize the potential of the Millennial knowledge worker.

- As I am given the flexibility to work independently, I become increasingly more productive and am more likely to collaborate with others, given the new time frames created by flexible parameters.
- Growth opportunities coupled with ways to actively contribute fuel the fire of ambition in many Millennials. These opportunity offerings motivate best if they are multidimensional.
- Most menial tasks may be worthwhile to a Millennial knowledge worker if there is an identifiable contribution to society.
- With many corporate initiatives and missions now including developmental and service-oriented relationships (working and being involved all at once), there is a clear effort to engage cause-oriented Millennial knowledge workers, like me.

The Millennial knowledge worker must recognize that employers are aware and willing to work with our differentiating attributes in order to keep us motivated. We possess the potential to sustain the competitive advantage sought in the corporate arena.

Develop Each Individual Employee

Nicole Hardin, Managing Director
HireStrategy

The most important steps any organization can take in developing a sustainable strategy for motivating and retaining Millennials is committing to their employees through strong management, focusing on the development of each individual. This generation craves responsibility and the ability to make an impact on the world around them. Ways to accomplish this include:

- Management that understands that their mission is to facilitate a meaningful relationship with these workers while leveraging their motivation and technical abilities.
- Strong organizational values, complemented by being socially conscientious and mission driven, will not only attract these workers but also earn their loyalty.
- It cannot be over-emphasized how critical it is that companies develop a transparent commitment not just to business values, but to society. It isn't enough anymore to "do no harm"; it is essential to be proactive in positive contribution to society.

This generation is looking for authenticity in all of the actions above, making the full commitment of the organization necessary to successfully motivate the Millennials.

Researchers Have Unique Needs

Deborah K. Hoover, Director of HR
The Urban Institute

It's really no secret—in our best young researchers, their motivation comes from within themselves.

- Avoid de-motivating them with heavy-handed supervision.
- Put your own ego aside and give true responsibility for a project.
- Teach and mentor by helping define problems and assignments.
- Relate real-world conditions to their work assignments.
- Listen, and employ patience.

Nurture the Millennial knowledge workers and get out of the way. They will make you proud and produce truly exceptional ideas and organizational results.

Pull Back the Motivational Lens and Manage Talent

Rick Humphress
Oracle Corporation

Organizations need to adapt their current talent management practices to accommodate Millennial employees. Leaders should:

- Create adequate career and succession plans that give Millennials a clear view of advancement.
- Recruit Millennials by using social networking methods, backed by a strong organizational brand and a streamlined staffing process.
- Motivate Millennials through a combination of monetary and non-monetary rewards that are tailored uniquely for each person.
- Develop Millennials using andragogical training delivered just in time as employees need them to be successful.
- Evaluate Millennials frequently and make the feedback bi-directional.

If organizations improve talent management along these lines, they will provide a smoother transition with a richer transfer of knowledge between generations.

Maximize Productivity and Commitment

Kris T. Jensen, VP Corporate Services
Wisdom Worker Solutions

In these competitive times, organizations are increasingly in need of a highly skilled but adaptable workforce. To develop the resources they require, leaders can influence Millennials' productivity and commitment by:

- Acknowledging their contributions and letting them participate in meaningful work projects that are aligned to the organization's mission and vision.
- Evaluating their performance based on business outcomes and results rather than on "face time"; allowing them to pioneer flexible alternatives to existing processes, schedules, and locations; and fearlessly innovating products and services.
- Communicating performance feedback, development activities, and career options on an informal, just-in-time basis.
- Leading from a position of influence, created through expertise, charisma, or information, rather than asserting organizational authority that will likely lead to compliance and resistance rather than engagement.
- Creating an employee value proposition that builds individual commitment to the organization long-term or welcomes them back when circumstances temporarily suspend the relationship.
- Modeling high-integrity business behaviors.

Imbued with confidence throughout their lives, Millennials will continue to push their environments to transition from control-based to freedom-based accountability and to share a mentality of free agency.

Understand that Millennials Play by Different Rules

Robert McGovern, CEO and Founder
Jobfox

Gen Y plays for a different set of rewards. Understanding this is the first step in motivating the Millennial knowledge worker:

- **More than money** — Gen Y isn't motivated by monetary rewards as much as older workers are. Young workers often value leisure time and flexible work schedule benefits, for example, more than money.
- **Experimentation** — Millennials are able to rapidly adapt to technology change via sophisticated trial-and-error learning styles. Employers must learn to accommodate and create organizational growth opportunities from these "learn-as-I go" approaches, across all business settings.
- **Contribution** — Top-down management hierarchies are foreign to the "Baby-on-Board" generation. From day one, corporate leaders must include Gen Y workers as significant participants in the establishment of business objectives and the roles to be played in meeting important corporate goals.
- **Stability** — Gen Y workers have grown up in a world filled with rapid change. As a result, they seek work as a refuge. However, very few companies are viewed as safe havens by Millennials.

This could be the most committed group of workers ever, I believe, but only for the companies that understand how to create favorable work environments for this new generation.

Learn from Millennials

Sue McLeod, Senior Consultant
Hay Group

The Millennial generation challenges the adult world they are joining because of their different approaches to work and their lives. We need to look beyond these challenges to see that these young people also have a lot of strengths, including their energy, education, and willingness to commit and work hard when the right situation is presented. The Millennial generation has a lot to offer, a lot to teach us, and a lot to learn. But didn't we all when we were their age? And more profoundly, don't we all, at every age?

By demanding (through their words and actions) more engaging work environments and more meaningful work, the Millennials are asking us to step up our leadership.

They come into work with the expectation that we will put the best practices into practice, rather than just paying lip service. The secret, though, is that the best practices will work for all of us, not just the Millennials.

By stepping up our leadership, we will also be teaching the Millennial generation how to lead. This will be a great gift to them and to the world, because the challenges they will face in their adult lives will be great—a changing economy and a changing global business landscape—and they'll eventually be leading the generations that follow them.

Provide Opportunities for Employee Growth

Kitty Nix, Director, Strategic Development
Helios HR

Millennials are often seeking employee development as a significant part of their employee/employer relationship. High-potential employees in this age group have increased expectations regarding their career growth and the responsibilities of their employers to provide appropriate opportunities. When motivating and working to retain Millennials, leaders must address these expectations and communicate the organization's plans and strategy in this area. Motivating this segment of your workforce through employee growth and development may include:

- Providing readily available, company-sponsored training and educational opportunities to keep skills sharp and current.
- Creating a well-defined career trajectory with both technical and management tracks that provide clear steps in career progression.
- Increasing communication between managers and employees regarding individual interests, future goals, and growth opportunities.

- Providing recognition for a job well done, a competitive salary that recognizes accomplishments, and identification of new challenges.
- Instituting a mentor program, providing coaching, and continually giving constructive feedback throughout the year.
- Ensuring that employees know how their contributions fit into the larger mission of the organization so they are not just executing a job description in isolation.
- Including Millennials in charting their own growth path, working to accommodate both personal and business goals.

Motivation for these individuals includes a partnership with an employer that is focused on experiential learning, continued skill growth, and a defined career path. The number-one priority of our Millennial workforce is being provided with multiple opportunities and avenues to develop to their full professional potential.

Customize the Employment Experience

Marcia Riley, Vice President, Talent Management and Human Resources
ESI International

I've learned from experience that it really is about creating a customized employment experience for everyone who joins your team. I try to treat my employees like valued *internal customers,* and the resulting ROI in loyalty and contribution is remarkable!

- The recruiting and on-boarding of Millennials begins at the interview. Once you know that you intend to make an offer, find out what the Millennial values in the arena of creativity, contribution, coaching, recognition, etc. Build choices into the way they get work done, and try to meet their needs from day one. Check in with them frequently about what is working and not working in their new position.
- Have them mentored by someone their age who has already made a successful transition into your organization. The research about employee engagement indicates that having even one friend at work increases the possibility that new employees will stay with the organization.
- Don't hover or micromanage; focus on results and deliverables.

In closing, remember that Millennial employees grew up in a different world than you did, but that world is just as real and critical to them as your world is to you. Recognize and respect their differences, and you'll have a wonderful new member of your multi-generational workforce.

One Size Does Not Fit All

Christopher R. Ryan, Deputy General Counsel
K12 Inc.

It is a mistake to apply a one-size-fits-all approach to motivating workers, especially Millennials. The key is to avoid the trap of assuming that what motivates you will apply equally to the employees you manage regardless of their age or function.

- New generations seek to distinguish themselves from prior generations to establish their own identity, and the Millennial generation of workers is no different.
- However, technology and the associated pace of change have made it more challenging for managers to adapt to and determine how to motivate this new group of workers.
- Today's manager needs to venture beyond his or her comfort zone to become more perceptive and open minded about meeting the needs of Millennial workers.
- Otherwise, it will be difficult to motivate and retain this group of workers, who are needed to perform staff work in the short term and who will become mid-level and senior managers in the long term.

Given the rapid growth of numerous economies through globalization, the future competitiveness of the United States depends on our ability to adapt to and leverage this next generation of workers.

Final Recommendations for Motivating Millennials

Kurt Schlimme, Project Management Office Director
The College Board

The new workforce of Millennials offers unknown potential related to performance, productivity, creativity, and innovation within their organizations. Managers must learn to harness this new potential through their management techniques.

- Defining specific work outcomes and time expectations in relation to assignments or deliverables allows Millennials to use their thought processes and work patterns in creative and effective manners.
- Letting them take ownership of the work products but governing the work products via constraints and expectations allows for the development of a natural mentoring relationship.
- Shifting managerial focus from "direct and control" to "observe and support" engages the workers' sense of commitment and contribution.

Millennials will be the new work force. Organizations that can adapt their cultures and management to optimize and motivate Millennial performance will be successful. Moreover, managers who can harness their potential and optimize Millennial performance will be highly recognized within their own organizations.

Address the Challenge of Motivating Millennial Knowledge Workers

Shira Harrington, Director, Professional Search Positions, Inc.

At the initial drafting of this book, our country had yet to be hit with the global economic recession we are currently facing. The impact of this downturn has been felt by most every worker, including Millennials. What was once the generation of What's-In-It-For-Me may be evolving into the generation of How-Do-I-Land-An-Unpaid-Internship?

The classic Howe and Strauss book *Generations* contends that every four generations we see the same generational traits recycle. This may be poignantly true for the Millennial generation, who, like their WWII elders, are learning to appreciate the little things once again. It will be interesting to watch the evolution of this generation, some of whom were in the workforce before the recession, some of whom are in college and facing an uncertain job market, and some of whom are sitting in classrooms and around the dinner table being prepared by their teachers and parents for a world with fewer pearls in their oysters.

All of that said, certain generational traits were imbued from an early age into the Millennials, and taught them that they could do anything they set their hearts and minds to and should settle for nothing less than the best in their careers. Blending their parental encouragement from the past with the financial uncertainty of the future should yield some interesting behavioral and motivational results for employers.

Hopefully, the lesson learned is that neither employer nor employee should take each other for granted any longer. Economic winds, societal events, and parenting styles may change, but we must learn to recognize that at the end of the day, businesses need to turn a profit and workers want to be appreciated for their contribution to the bottom line. Focusing on what motivates every employee makes good sense for Wall Street—and for Main Street.

Leverage Unique Motivators

Mark Steffanina, Director of Organizational Effectiveness
Holy Cross Hospital

Leveraging the unique motivations of Millennial knowledge workers fosters their engagement, providing an environment conducive to eliciting their discretionary effort. Consequently, engaging environments that draw on knowledge worker motivations fuel outcomes such as employee satisfaction, retention, and productivity.

- Understand and recognize that knowledge worker motivational factors can serve as keys to unlocking performance potential.
- Use the Team Improvement and Prioritization Matrix (TIP'M) methodology to involve twenty-something knowledge workers in evaluating their workplaces.
- Employ the completed TIP'M to identify misalignment between motivational factors and workplace characteristics.
- Encourage knowledge worker participation in action plan development and implementation to realize the latent opportunities identified by the TIP'M.

Having twenty-something knowledge workers contribute to building their motivation-leveraging workplace will provide not only a satisfying working environment but also improved organizational performance.

Foster Employee Commitment and Engagement

Hector Velez, Executive Vice President, Business Development
HireStrategy

Employers in the Washington, D.C. metro area, one of the most vibrant employment markets in the country, look to HireStrategy as a value-added resource in order to design and implement their human capital initiatives. This has opened a privileged window into the inner workings of some of the great places to work and some of the not-so-great places to work in our country. Those great places to work have definitely figured out how to create the conditions that allow their staffs to succeed and achieve their professional, financial, and personal goals. The following includes some of our observations.

Employee commitment and engagement are key to any organizations success. The Millennial generation requires that management rethink their leadership styles and focus. Now, more than ever, leaders need to:

- Create a culture where everybody is a customer who needs to be delighted; "everybody" includes employees, support staff, paying customers, job applicants, and the community at large.
- Demonstrate a strong sense of humility (the era of know-it-alls is over).

- Communicate with total transparency, from the strategic to the tactical, within all functional areas, especially the financial (the era of surprises is over).
- Avoid delusional optimism or the purposeful ignorance of the facts, which will be counterproductive when the realities of the business world and the economy at large inevitable disrupt a company's "hockey stick" growth curve!
- Lead by example in order to create and promote a culture of complete trust and confidence where employees are treated like mature professional adults (the era of micromanagement is over).
- Avoid overreliance on managing to quarterly earnings, which has hollowed out organizations' leadership ranks. Hopefully we are entering a new era of truly enlightened organizational design and economic vibrancy.

Organizations—whether private-sector firms, publicly traded firms, government agencies, or nonprofits—need to embrace a paradigm shift from managing by numbers to managing talent.

Use Technology Challenges as Motivators

Stuart H. Weinstein, Ph.D, Senior Managing Consultant
IBM

Motivation for 21–30-year-old knowledge workers is no longer merely grounded in their potential salary, long-term commitments to an employer, or assurances of sequential progression in a specific field. It's critical to recognize that:

- Technology challenges, the potential to be "special," and opportunities to contribute generate motivation within the employee and spark enthusiasm in the job environment, which is rewarding when it spreads to others at any age.
- At high-tech firms, satisfaction often comes from Millennials' personal accomplishments and the ability to experiment with new ideas and products that are perceived as a vision for their future.
- Technology and innovation may not permit "seasoning" of their ideas, but rather require rapid adoption.
- Employers should harness the excitement that the Millennials feel and encourage them to communicate it to those who are entering the workforce.

The ability of the Millennials to be unconstrained by tradition, and allowed to explore new ideas and combinations of ideas that have never been considered, encourages them to influence what is yet to be our future.

Chapter Checklist: Designing Your Action Plan

The following learning objectives appeared in previous chapters. Review and select those that are relevant to designing your own plan for motivating Millennials.

Introduction: Understanding the Millennial Knowledge Worker

- ☐ 1. Review five recommendations for using this book effectively.
- ☐ 2. Gain an understanding of the Millennial knowledge worker.
- ☐ 3. Share responsibility for motivating the Millennial knowledge worker.

Introduction: Millennial Motivational Issues

- ☐ 1. Acknowledge broader Millennial motivational issues.
- ☐ 2. Appreciate four portraits of Millennials from Contributing Experts' perspective.
- ☐ 3. Understand the critical Millennial motivational factors that drive this book.

Part 1: Flexibility and Work/Life Balance

- ☐ 1. Acknowledge the importance of flexibility and work/life balance.
- ☐ 2. Explore flexible work arrangements driven by the current workforce crisis.
- ☐ 3. Take a closer look at Millennials' need for flexibility and work/life balance.
- ☐ 4. Develop proactive strategies in support of flexibility and work/life balance.

CONTINUED

CONTINUED

Part 2: Multidimensional Millennial Growth Opportunities

- ❑ 1. Recognize that multidimensional growth opportunities are non-negotiable Millennial requirements.
- ❑ 2. Reconcile growth opportunities of Millennials and the intellectual-capital needs of knowledge organizations.
- ❑ 3. Consider the multidimensional Millennial growth opportunities presented by Contributing Experts.
- ❑ 4. Identify Millennial leadership opportunities through growth opportunities.

Part 3: Fun and Social Interaction

- ❑ 1. Harness the importance of fun and social interaction as a significant Millennial motivational factor as well as a valued human capital asset.
- ❑ 2. Encourage managers and human resources professionals to incorporate strategies for adding fun into the workplace.
- ❑ 3. Identify opportunities to incorporate social interaction into the workplace.

Part 4: Purpose, Contribution, and Challenging Work

- ❑ 1. Provide flexible opportunities to meet Millennials' need for career and life purpose.
- ❑ 2. Recognize the contribution that Millennials make to their workplaces and society.
- ❑ 3. Address Millennials' need for challenging work that addresses global, national, and organizational issues.

Part 5: Establishing and Sustaining Effective Communication

- ❑ 1. Establish and sustain effective communication that meets Millennial motivational needs.
- ❑ 2. Acknowledge that effective communication is a shared responsibility of manager and Millennial.
- ❑ 3. Employ a variety of relevant communication strategies and tactics.

CONTINUED

CONTINUED

Part 6: The Three Rs: Recognition, Rewards, and Respect

- ❑ 1. Identify the unique generational factors that influence the importance of recognition, rewards, and respect as Millennial motivators.
- ❑ 2. Appreciate the importance of appropriate recognition for Millennial knowledge workers.
- ❑ 3. Establish an organizational and managerial climate to apply reward strategies.
- ❑ 4. Develop a mutually beneficial climate in support of respect.

Part 7: Learning, Training, and Technology

- ❑ 1. Understand the forces shaping America's economy and their implications for work and workers in the 21st century.
- ❑ 2. Recognize that knowledge has become the critically important factor in economic life.
- ❑ 3. Respond to the paradigm shift from 20th-century training to 21st-century learning.
- ❑ 4. Appreciate the Millennials' unique learning preferences.

Part 8: Pay for Performance

- ❑ 1. Include the tangible motivator of money as a driver of superior performance.
- ❑ 2. Move beyond the traditional concept of a performance appraisal to implement a pay-for-performance system.
- ❑ 3. Identify strategies for providing financial rewards for knowledge.
- ❑ 4. Implement pay-for-performance initiatives in shorter time frames (12–36 months).

An Organizational Millennial Motivational Assessment

The primary focus of this book has been encouraging individual managers and human resources professionals to assume responsibility for developing and motivating Millennial knowledge workers. In Appendix 2, Contributing Expert Mark Steffanina presents a methodology that provides an opportunity for organizations to take responsibility for conducting a motivational factors survey to effect broader change. First, an explanation of the Team Improvement and Prioritizing Matrix methodology is presented. Second, examples of its application are presented to illustrate its effectiveness.

Introducing the TIP'M Methodology

Mark Steffanina, MBA, Director of Organizational Effectiveness, Holy Cross Hospital

Disciplined problem solving, continuous improvement, and data-driven decision making form an integral part of organizational development activity, particularly as they provide for the weaving of unique human insights into the fabric of organizational functioning. One approach, both tactical and strategic, to build a pro-Millennial workplace is to use a disciplined technique known as the Team Improvement and Prioritization Matrix (TIP'M) methodology. The TIP'M methodology uses motivational criteria to assess organizational health by performing a gap analysis of the organization's current state and one that encourages Millennial motivation.

The TIP'M enables organizational development practitioners to transform the workplace into one that is Millennial oriented by maximizing and leveraging their unique motivational factors. Leveraging the factors of Millennial motivation in organizational design fosters Millennial recruitment, development, and retention—strategic objectives pursued by many organizations interested in human capital. Moreover, using Millennial motivational factors to shape the Millennial workplace ultimately pays dividends to the organization in terms of improved outcomes attained through encouraging Millennial performance and productivity.

The TIP'M methodology also serves as a tactical device, directly engaging and involving Millennials in the process of organizational development. In so doing, the TIP'M methodology is an empowering tool, facilitating Millennial participation in workplace improvement. Engaging Millennials in a direct manner, making them collaborators in the enhancement of workplace functioning, serves to engender a sense of ownership among them and fosters their connection to the organizational enhancements that will result from the use of the methodology. In addition, by engendering ownership, the TIP'M methodology leads to the promotion of Millennial discretionary effort, driving their retention and further encouraging their performance and productivity.

Determining Priorities

Social psychological factors, group dynamics, and organizational culture and health all affect the way in which Millennials perceive their motivational factors. The first stage in building a Team Improvement and Prioritization Matrix (TIP'M) is to determine how the Millennials in a particular organization perceive the priority of the various Millennial motivational factors. These priorities will serve the organizational development practitioner by indicating the degree of influence that each factor has on the organization's Millennial workforce. Pursuant to building a working environment that facilitates Millennial motivation, these factors become characteristics or necessary criteria of a motivational workplace. Consequently, the priority that a particular Millennial subgroup places on one factor over another becomes a rather important key to an organizational development practitioner.

There are many ways to determine the priorities that a particular Millennial group places on various motivational factors; the critical aspect of ranking the factors is the engagement of the Millennials in the activity. If it is possible to physically assemble the group, then brainstorming, multi-voting, Crawford slips, and nominal group techniques can be used to involve the Millennials in ranking their motivational factors. In organizations with a technological orientation, online surveys, shared databases, virtual bulletin boards, e-mail, or even text messages can be used to collect input from the Millennial subgroup and rank their motivational factors.

The ranked motivational factors form the left, or vertical, axis of the TIP'M (Figure 1) and will be used as weighted criteria against which the organization will be assessed. These will ultimately direct an organizational development practitioner to the gaps between the organization's current state and one that promotes Millennial motivation.

The factors may be prioritized in various ways. Perhaps the easiest approach may be to have each Millennial rank the factors in order from most significant to least so the organizational development practitioner can aggregate and weight them accordingly. Another method may involve the use of a Likert scale, having each Millennial provide his or her perception of the degree of influence that each motivational factor has in order for the organizational development practitioner to subsequently use the average response for each motivational factor's weight.

Describing the Organization within a TIP'M

The second stage in building a Millennial-focused workplace with the TIP'M methodology is the construction of the top, or, horizontal axis of the matrix (Figure 1). Along the horizontal axis are descriptors, characteristics, activities, or features of the workplace in its current state. These descriptive characteristics of the current workplace may include, for example, flexible scheduling, weekly staff meetings, on-site educational opportunities, recognition events, merit compensation increases, and so on, depending on the organization. Refer to the end of this section for examples of workplace features used to construct Team Improvement and Priority Matrices.

Assessing Organizational Characteristics Against Motivational Factors

The third stage in developing a TIP'M and using it for workplace transformation is to assess each of the organizational characteristics against the Millennial motivational factors. This stage involves the Millennials in evaluating their workplace in terms of its ability to respond to their motivational factors. The Millennials will compare each characteristic of their workplace against their motivational factors and will assign a rating indicating how well the workplace characteristic responds or supports each motivational factor.

A rating system of some sort is employed to describe these relationships; variations may include scales of 1–3 (corresponding to ordinal responses such as Low, Medium, or High), or gradients of 1–5 or 1–10; and 0 for no relationship or support at all. Common among these rating systems is that the higher number corresponds to a greater link between the workplace feature or characteristic and the motivational factor.

For example, should flexible scheduling be a feature of a particular workplace, each Millennial would evaluate it against each motivational factor, expressing his or her perspective by using the defined scale. One would expect an organizational characteristic such as flexible scheduling to be highly responsive to the Millennial motivational factor of flexibility. However, if this characteristic is perceived by the particular group of Millennials as something other than highly responsive, such feedback would be an important cue to the organizational development practitioner of an opportunity in distributive, procedural, or transactional justice or some other issue that may impede flexible scheduling.

Just as with engaging the Millennial subgroup in ranking their motivational factors, having them assess features of their workplace may be done in a wide variety of ways. Some organizations may prefer assembling their Millennials together in a focus group, while others may prefer to collect each individual Millennial's response in the form of an online or paper survey. Of course, if some survey method is used, the organizational development practitioner will have to aggregate the responses in some manner. No matter how the Millennials are engaged in the process, the organizational development practitioner will benefit from their insight, feedback, and ownership in honing their workplace into an environment that contributes to their motivation.

Completing the TIP'M

The fourth stage in employing the TIP'M methodology and transforming the workplace into one supporting Millennial motivation is the completion of the matrix. The weights assigned by the Millennials to each of their motivational factors are considered against their ratings of each workplace feature. Although there are several ways to compare the workplace features and corresponding motivational factors, one robust approach is to represent the weight of each motivational factor relative to the responsiveness of each workplace feature by the product of the two measures. In other words, the matrix is completed by multiplying each motivational factor's rank by each corresponding workplace feature's rating, indicating the product in the cell adjacent to the feature's rating, as shown in Figure 1.

Team Improvement and Prioritization Matrix©

Relative Rank	Motivational Factors	Workplace Feature 1		Workplace Feature 2	
(Slightly Motivating = 1 Highly Motivating = 10)	Evaluate each workplace feature against these motivational factors below on a 1 - 10 scale in terms of how well they respond to each motivational factor. 1= Little responsiveness, 10= High responsiveness. Use '0' to indicate no responsiveness whatsoever.	Flexible Scheduling		Weekly Staff Meetings	
10	**Flexibility**	10	100	3	30
9	**Fun**	2	18	6	54
8	**Rewards and Recognition**	2	16	6	48
7	**Challenge**	0	0	1	7

Figure 1: Sample matrix view

The TIP'M is completed by calculating the sum of the products of each column and row. In the previous example, the sum of the products in the Flexible Scheduling column is 134, and the sum of the products in the Weekly Staff Meetings column is 139. Comparing the sums of all the columns will help you understand which workplace features tend to provide greater support for Millennial motivation over others. Similarly, the row sums may also be calculated to provide insight into how the motivational factors are encouraged by the workplace features.

Analysis of the Completed Matrix

The fifth stage in using the TIP'M method to improve organizational functioning by leveraging Millennial motivations is to analyze the completed matrix. Having engaged the Millennial subgroup in the process of developing the TIP'M, the organizational development practitioner has rich feedback to guide organizational improvement. The completed matrix may be used in several ways; among the most obvious is to note the cells with the highest and lowest products. In the Figure 1 example, Flexibility relative to Flexible Scheduling received the highest rating, suggesting its high relative responsiveness to the Millennial motivator of flexibility. Conversely, Challenge relative to Flexible Scheduling received the lowest rating, signifying a lack of responsiveness between the workplace feature, Flexible Scheduling, and the Millennial motivator, Challenge. It is important to note that this lack of responsiveness may not necessarily be a negative aspect of organizational functioning (as perhaps the two cannot, or should not, be related). However, these relationships are noteworthy when the entire matrix is viewed from a broad perspective rather than a cellular one.

One broader perspective is to analyze these results across each motivational-factor row. In Figure 1, doing so might suggest that the Challenge motivational factor is not well addressed by the workplace features in general, receiving only "0" and "1" for a row sum of "7" from the Millennial subgroup.

The results of tallying the high and low aggregate ratings given by the Millennials provide a sense of what generally responds to their motivating factors and what does not, another way to consider the results. No matter which analytical perspective or combination thereof is used, the results of the TIP'M methodology are helpful in guiding future organizational development efforts aimed at bolstering Millennial motivation.

Sharing Results

A final stage in the use of the TIP'M methodology, as with any disciplined improvement method that engages people in the improvement process, is to share the results with the Millennials involved and suggest subsequent next steps. Since the Millennial subgroup was actively involved in the process of creating the TIP'M, they rightly deserve a review of the finished product. Sharing subsequent next steps to be taken organizationally in response to their input into the TIP'M will further promote their ownership of the improvements to come, increasing their motivation to contribute.

Team Improvement and Prioritization Matrix©

Relative Rank (Slightly Motivating = 1 Highly Motivating = 10)	Motivational Factors Evaluate each workplace feature against these motivational factors below on a 1 - 10 scale in terms of how well they respond to each motivational factor. 1= Little responsiveness, 10= High responsiveness. Use '0' to indicate no responsiveness whatsoever.	Workplace Feature 1 Flexible Scheduling	Workplace Feature 2 Weekly Staff Meetings	Workplace Feature 3 Monthly Service Awards	Workplace Feature 4 Onsite Training	Workplace Feature 5 Quarterly Teambuilding Event	Total	Factor Responsiveness Quotient
10	**Flexibility**	10 / 100	3 / 30	4 / 40	6 / 60	3 / 30	260	52%
9	**Fun**	2 / 18	6 / 54	8 / 72	8 / 72	10 / 90	306	68%
8	**Rewards and Recognition**	2 / 16	6 / 48	10 / 80	5 / 40	8 / 64	248	62%
7	**Challenge**	0 / 0	1 / 7	1 / 7	6 / 42	9 / 63	119	34%
6	Pay for Performance	3 / 18	3 / 18	4 / 24	5 / 30	2 / 12	102	34%
5	**Respect**	5 / 25	8 / 40	9 / 45	7 / 35	8 / 40	185	74%
4	Communication	8 / 32	10 / 40	3 / 12	6 / 24	8 / 32	140	70%
3	Social Interaction	2 / 6	7 / 21	9 / 27	5 / 15	9 / 27	96	64%
2	Purpose and/or Contribution	5 / 10	7 / 14	8 / 16	4 / 8	9 / 18	66	66%
1	Technology	8 / 8	3 / 3	3 / 3	9 / 9	2 / 2	25	50%
	Total	233	275	326	335	378		
	Feature Responsiveness Quotient	45%	54%	59%	61%	68%		

M. Steffanina, 2008

Figure 2: Team Improvement and Prioritization Matrix, Sample 1

TEAM PRIORITIZATION AND IMPROVEMENT MATRIX©		Sporting Events	Career Development Planning	Staff Meetings	Performance Reports	Educational Programs	Quarterly Goal Celebrations	Holiday Celebrations	Fitness Program		Responsiveness Quotient
MOTIVATING FACTORS	Relative Importance	Responsiveness for each feature above (scale: L for Low, M for Medium, H for High)									
Respect	8.8	M	M	L	L	M	M	L	L		0%
Communication	8.1	L	L	H	H	M	L	L	L		25%
Social Interaction	7.8	H	L	L	L	L	H	H	M		38%
Purpose and/or Contribution	7.6	L	M	M	L	L	H	H	L		25%
Rewards and Recognition	7.4	L	L	L	L	L	H	H	L		25%
Challenge	7.3	H	L	L	L	H	L	L	M		25%
Fun	7.2	H	L	L	L	L	H	H	M		38%
Flexibility	7.2	L	L	L	L	L	L	L	L		0%
Pay for Performance	6.3	L	M	L	M	M	L	L	L		0%
Technology	6.0	L	M	L	L	M	L	L	L		0%
	Total Low	6	6	8	8	5	5	6	7	Total Responsiveness Quotient	
	Total Medium	1	4	1	1	4	1	0	3		
	Total High	3	0	1	1	1	4	4	0	18%	
	Aggregate Responsiveness	-3	-6	-7	-7	-4	-1	-2	-7		

M. Steffanina, 2008

Figure 3: Team Improvement and Prioritization Matrix, Sample 2

Team Improvement and Prioritization Matrix©	Factor Rank	Staff Development Opportunities	Factor Weight	Comp Time	Factor Weight	Support from Supervision	Factor Weight	Interaction with co-workers	Factor Weight	Interaction with scholars	Factor Weight	Total Characteristic Score	Factor Weighted Responsiveness Ratio
Communication	10	3	30	3.5	35	4.5	45	3.5	35	4	40	185	74%
Respect	9	4	36	3	27	3.5	31.5	3.5	31.5	4.5	40.5	166.5	74%
Pay for Performance	8	2	16	1.5	12	1.5	12	1.5	12	1.5	12	64	32%
Purpose and/or Contribution	7	2.5	17.5	2.5	17.5	2.5	17.5	3.5	24.5	5	35	112	64%
Social Interaction	6	1.5	9	3.5	21	3.5	21	3.5	21	5	30	102	68%
Learning	5	2.5	12.5	2	10	2.5	12.5	4	20	5	25	80	64%
Challenging Environment	4	4	16	3.5	14	4.5	18	3	12	4.5	18	78	78%
Flexibility	3	3.5	10.5	4	12	4	12	4	12	5	15	61.5	82%
Technology	2	4	8	2	4	3.5	7	3	6	5	10	35	70%
Fun	1	3.5	3.5	4	4	4	4	3.5	3.5	5	5	20	80%
Total Aspect Score		30.5	159	29.5	156.5	34	180.5	33	177.5	44.5	230.5	**66%**	
Responsiveness Ratio		61%		59%		68%		66%		89%		**Factor Weighted Assessment Score**	

M. Steffanina, 2008

Figure 4: Team Improvement and Prioritization Matrix, Sample 3

Viva-Crisp 50-Minute
Titles in the Series

ISBN	Author	Title	YOP	Price
9788130918174	Gambino	**50 Minutes to Better Software Demos**: *Apply Your Sales Skills with Confidence*	2011	195.00
9788130918488	Bozek	**50 One-Minute Tips to Better Communications**: *Speak, Write and Present More Effectively, 3/e*	2011	250.00
9788130918211	Conlow & Watsabaugh	**Achieving Supervisory Excellence**: *Be the Leader Your People Need*	2011	195.00
9788130918396	McKnight & Chapman	**Attitude**: *Protect Your Most Priceless Asset, 5/e*	2011	245.00
9788130918495	Terry Dickey	**Basics of Budgeting**: *Become a Better Business Planner, 2/e*	2011	250.00
9788130918310	Conlow & Watsabaugh	**Become a Successful Supervisor**: *Develop Essential People Skills*	2011	225.00
9788130918327	Brock	**Better Business Writing**: *Become A More Powerful Communicator, 5/e*	2011	225.00
9788130918228	Dupont	**Business Etiquette & Professionalism**: *Conduct Yourself With Confidence, 3/e*	2011	195.00
9788130918181	Morgan	**Calming Upset Customers**: *Stay in Control ... In any Situation, 4/e*	2011	195.00
9788130918198	Minor	**Coaching and Counseling**: *Become a Better Manager Through Mentoring, 4/e*	2011	195.00
9788130918273	Decker	**Communication Skills for Leaders**: *Deliver a Clear and Consistent Message, 4/e*	2011	225.00
9788130918143	Kindler	**Conflict Management**: *Resolve Disagreement at Work, 4/e*	2011	165.00
9788130918280	Conlow & Watsabaugh	**Creating a High Performance Team**: *Gain the Skills of Today's Successful Leaders*	2011	225.00
9788130918334	Feldman	**Critical Thinking**: *Make Strategic Decisions With Confidence, 2/e*	2011	225.00
9788130918426	Flynn	**E-Mail Management**: *Keep Your Inbox Under Control, 2/e*	2011	245.00
9788130918471	Kravitz & Schubert	**Emotional Intelligence Works**: *Think, Be and Work Smarter, 3/e*	2011	245.00
9788130918150	Maddux	**Ethics in Business**: *Manage With Authority and Fairness, 2/e*	2011	195.00
9788130918235	Rouillard	**Goals and Goal Setting**: *Achieve Measurable Results, 4/e*	2011	195.00
9788130918204	Conlow Watsabaugh	**Handling Difficult People and Situations**: *Lead People Through Adversity*	2011	195.00

ISBN	Author	Title	YOP	Price
9788130918433	Wendover	**High Performance Hiring**: *Select the Best Every Time, 3/e*	2011	245.00
9788130918402	Shea	**Making the Most of Being Mentored**: *Mentors Help Mentees Do, 2/e*	2011	245.00
9788130918242	Scott	**Managing Personal Change**: *Stay Positive and Stay in Control*, 3/e	2011	195.00
9788130918341	Haynes	**Meeting Skills for Leaders**: *Make Meetings More Productive, 4/e*	2011	225.00
9788130918440	Shea	**Mentoring**: *Make It A Mutually Rewarding Experience, 4/e*	2011	245.00
9788130918525	Shandler	**Motivating the Millennial Knowledge Worker**: *Help Today's Workforce Succeed in Today's Economy*	2011	395.00
9788130918167	Mandel	**Presentation Skills**: *Captivate and Educate Your Audience, 4/e*	2011	195.00
9788130918518	Pokras	**Problem Solving for Teams**: *Make Consensus More Achievable, 3/e*	2011	295.00
9788130918259	Haynes	**Project Management**: *Get from the Idea to Implementation Successfully, 4/e*	2011	195.00
9788130918372	Martin	**Quality Customer Service**: *Satisfy Customers–It's Everybody's Job, 5/e*	2011	245.00
9788130918457	Lightle & Doucet	**Sexual Harassment in the Workplace**: *Create a Better Workplace For Everyone, 3/e*	2011	245.00
9788130918501	Lengefeld	**Study Skills Strategies**: *Get the Most From Every Minute of Learning, 4/e*	2011	250.00
9788130918358	Conlow & Watsabaugh	**SuperSTAR Customer Service**: *It's all about C.A.R.E.*	2011	225.00
9788130918297	Maddux & Wingfield	**Team Building**: *Turn Personal Strengths Into Group Success, 5/e*	2011	225.00
9788130918464	Finch	**Telephone Courtesy & Customer Service**: *Be Your Company's Lifeline to Customers, 4/e*	2011	245.00
9788130918389	Conlow & Watsabaugh	**Telephone Skills that Satisfy Customers**: *Unleash the Full Potential of the Telephone*	2011	245.00
9788130918303	Romero	**The Business of Listening**: *Become a More Effective Listener, 4/e*	2011	225.00
9788130918365	Chapman & McKnight	**The New Supervisor**: *Lead With Confidence, 5/e*	2011	225.00
9788130918266	Haynes	**Time Management**: *Get An Extra Day a Week*	2011	195.00
9788130918419	Gill & Chatton	**Understanding Financial Statements**: *Master the Tools That Help You Succeed, 3/e*	2011	245.00